day trips® from
new york city

first edition

getaway ideas for the local traveler

shandana a. durrani

917.471
D

travel

Guilford, Connecticut

All the information in this guidebook is subject to change. We recommend that you call ahead to obtain current information before traveling.

To buy books in quantity for corporate use
or incentives, call **(800) 962-0973**
or e-mail **premiums@GlobePequot.com**.

Editor: Amy Lyons
Project Editor: Heather Santiago
Layout: Joanna Beyer
Text Design: Linda R. Loiewski
Maps: Design Maps Inc. © Morris Book Publishing, LLC.
Spot photography throughout © Nancy Kennedy/Shutterstock

ISBN 978-0-7627-6460-0

Printed in the United States of America
10 9 8 7 6 5 4 3 2 1

contents

about the author

Shandana A. Durrani has been a magazine editor and writer in New York City for 19 years and has lived in New York City since 1993. Her work has appeared in numerous publications, including *Condé Nast Traveler, Glamour, Cigar Aficionado, Wine Spectator,* NYMag .com, *Haute Living, Silverkris, Refined Living,* Justluxe.com, Jetsetter.com and Simonseeks .com. You can reach her at www.shandanaadurrani.com.

acknowledgments

Quite a few people have helped me cull information for this guide and I can't thank them enough.

Thanks to Susan Hawvermale at Orange County Tourism. You provided me with invaluable information on Port Jervis, Barryville, and Mountainville. Too bad the Falun Gong retreat doesn't allow visitors. Thanks to Spark Creative and Cass Duffey in Collingswood, New Jersey; John Alexander in Burlington, New Jersey; Lydia Higginson in Dutchess County, New York; Carol Beder at Hearstrings in Clinton, New Jersey; Amy Hollander and Joe Eggert at the Red Mill Museum in Clinton, New Jersey; Joe Degand in Haddonfield, New Jersey; Sal at New Jersey Tourism; Andrea at the North Fork Promotion Council in Long Island; and Eric Scheffel at Empire State Development.

Thanks to my friends who drove around with me and/or provided valuable insight on towns I should and shouldn't include: Melissa Bowling, Jennifer Wells Gorman, Veronica Chambers, and most importantly, Kimberly Tryba. Kimberly, I can't thank you enough for all your help, especially for escorting me to many of the towns in the guide. It wasn't just work for me having you as my companion on our day trips through six different towns a day, and meeting lovable Riley was a bonus.

Thanks to my good friend and fellow "Day Trips" author, Sandra Ramani. Your advice, encouragement and loyal friendship have been invaluable.

Thanks to my wonderful family. Mummy and Baba, I know I was a complete pain in the neck while writing this book. Thank you for being such kind, loving, and understanding people and giving me the space I needed to get this done. You've supported my every endeavor and have always had faith in my abilities. I am honored to be your daughter and I love you. Thank you, Tooba and Navera for your support and encouragement and sisterly advice. Tooba, I appreciate you encouraging breaks when I visited you in Portland while writing this guide. Thanks most of all to Dames. You're the glue that holds me together, and your support and understanding have been invaluable.

Finally, thanks to my editor, Amy Lyons. You gave me breathing room and positive reinforcement throughout the long and arduous research and writing process. That means a lot.

introduction

From antique havens to strenuous hiking trails to charming colonial towns to pristine white sand beaches to contemporary art meccas, the New York City quad-state area has a lot to offer anyone looking to escape the hustle and bustle of the city for a day.

To the north of the city, you'll find enticing small towns known for antiques shopping and contemporary art museums. Hiking aficionados will delight in the miles of scenic trails in the Catskills and Northwestern Connecticut, some of which are the toughest in the region. (Make sure you don't get caught hiking down a mountain in the dark as I did in the fall of 2009. Scary doesn't cover it.) Fall foliage seekers can't skip the Litchfield Hills, often cited as the best place in the Northeast at which to see the changing seasons. Standing atop a peak on the Appalachian Trail, one can't adequately describe the riotous color display. Wine lovers will enjoy a trip to the lesser-known Hudson Valley wineries, some of which are the oldest vineyards in the country. Ghost hunters can hit the towns of Tarrytown and Sleepy Hollow as well as overgrown ruins, dilapidated icons, and deserted cultural treasures in Ulster, Dutchess, Rockland, and Putnam Counties.

South of the City, on the way to Philadelphia, lie towns steeped in Quaker traditions, many of which still hold firm. These towns have retained their historic flavor while becoming culinary and/or shopping destinations. Some of the towns are well known to day trippers, but you'll also discover hidden gems with manufacturing pasts that somehow offer miles of bucolic beauty as well as friendly locals always happy to lend a hand or offer a suggestion on where to eat or stay. Driving along the beautiful Delaware Raritan canal can be a day trip in and of itself and you may not even want to park the car. Philadelphia, like New York, is a city steeped in history that has a wealth of world-class museums, beautiful Beaux Arts buildings, and venues at which to enjoy good food and good music. Unfortunately, all the sites couldn't be listed.

To the west are outdoor sculpture meccas, towns with tons of ethnic flavor and romantic villages time seems to have forgotten. Some are so small you'd blink and miss them. But they are worth a side trip if for nothing else than the chance to detox, breath in the fresh air, and take in the beautiful vistas. At one noted site, you can be in three states at once. The drive can be one of the prettiest from the city, through rolling hills and wildflower-laden meadowland. Make sure to take a detour to the truss bridges of Hunterdon County and stop at one of the many farm stands along the way.

Heading east, you'll find seaside resort towns with beautiful marinas, posh eateries, and lodgings and historic estates that rival those in Europe. Not every town is chichi, however, some are decidedly middle class with a truly welcoming vibe, especially for

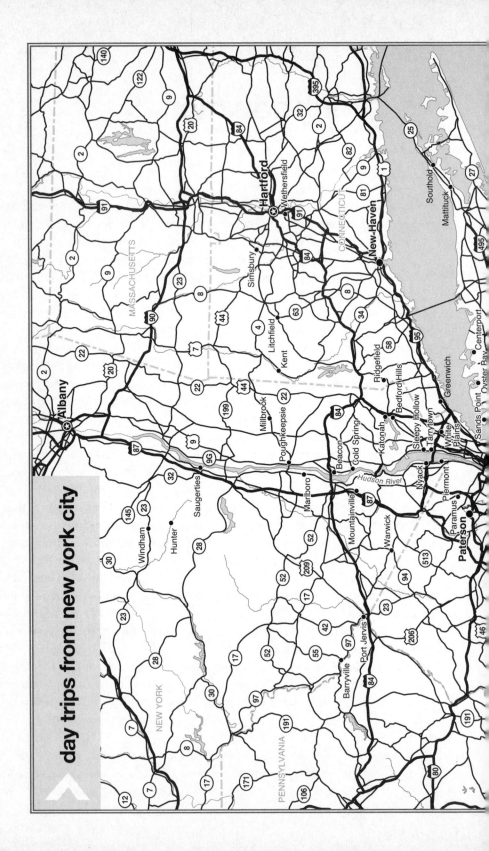

day trips from new york city

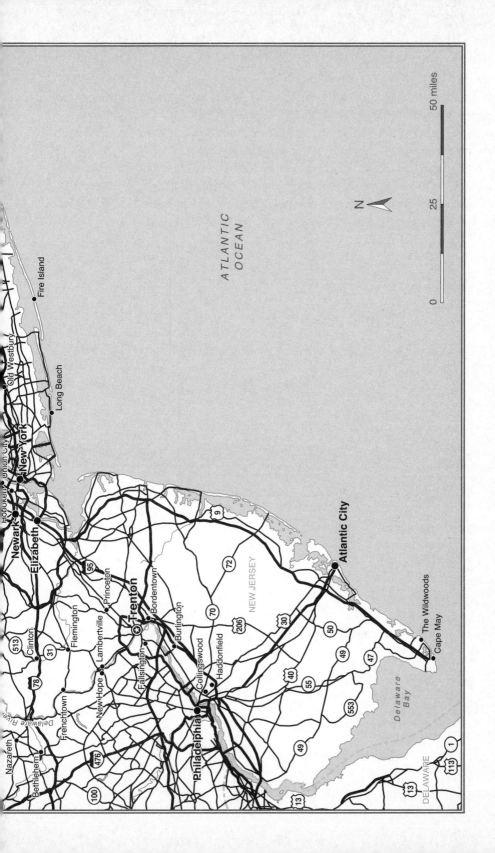

weekenders looking for a low-key beach getaway. Others are historic havens for gay, lesbian, and transgendered people, at which everyone is welcome as long as you leave your prejudices at home. Don't forget a trip to the lovely North Fork for the world-class wine. It's a romantic getaway that seems to get more popular each year.

New York City and the surrounding environs offer a wealth of fun-filled day trips for active-minded travelers and those wanting a relaxing getaway far from the stress of city life. The tri-state area and Pennsylvania offer pleasing respites for anyone with a car or a train or bus ticket looking for something new or familiar, but less traveled.

using this guide

Day Trips from New York City is organized by general direction from the city—north, south, east, west, northeast, northwest, and southwest—to points in the Tri-state area and Pennsylvania. Listings in the Where to Go, Where to Shop, Where to Eat, and Where to Stay sections are arranged in alphabetical order, unless otherwise specified. Each stop on every day trip includes a Where to Go listing, but Where to Shop, Where to Eat, and Where to Stay are only included when there are appropriate listings worth visiting. It is up to you where you want to spend your time, but *Day Trips* highlights the best a town or area has to offer. Plenty of overnight options are provided for those looking to make a quick trip a little longer.

scheduling your trip

Summer is peak season for most of the destinations in this guide, especially seaside and beach towns. Northwestern Connecticut and the upper Hudson Valley are more popular in the fall. Some of the best times to see some of the towns in this guide are in the early winter and late spring, before and after many tourists have come and gone. Eastern Long Island can be a lovely place when the snow blankets the ground and deals can be had during this time due to it being low season. For fall foliage, head northeast to Connecticut and upstate New York late in October. It's a little after peak, but you'll still enjoy the colors and avoid the crowds. The beach is great before Memorial Day and can still be enjoyed through the end of September. Lifeguards are off-duty and you can enjoy the water, albeit at your own risk. For surfers, this is a particularly great time to enjoy quiet beaches and even more secluded waves. April and May are also great months at which to enjoy some rural New Jersey, New York, and Pennsylvania towns as festivals run year-round and you're more likely to meet friendly locals and enjoy a great restaurant without having to vie with others for a choice seat.

hours of operation, prices & credit cards

We've provided details on hours, pricing, and credit cards as they were at the time of publication. In the interest of accuracy and because they are subject to change, hours of operation and attraction prices are given in general terms. Always remember to call ahead.

You can assume all establishments listed accept major credit cards unless otherwise noted. If you have questions, contact the establishment for specifics.

pricing key

restaurants

The pricing key reflects the average price for a single dinner entree, excluding cocktails, wine, appetizers, desserts, tax, and tip. Most restaurants are less expensive during breakfast, brunch, and lunch, which are good options should you choose a more popular or highly rated eatery. Some of the establishments are BYOB, which significantly reduces the cost of a night out. Some of the high-end eateries offer tasting menus, which feature a considerable amount of food for a good price.

$ Less than $12
$$ $12 to $25
$$$ More than $25

accommodations

The pricing key reflects the average cost of a one-night stay in a standard room for two adults during high season. Prices don't include sales tax, occupancy tax, or any other additional charges and fees. Discounts may apply for senior citizens, members of the military, war veterans, AAA members, and for extended stays. Check with each establishment for its policy.

$ Less than $120
$$ $120 to $175
$$$ More than$175

driving tips

So you're renting a car and driving out of the city rather than taking the train. That's the first challenge. Getting out of Manhattan can take time, especially if you do it during rush hour, on a Friday afternoon, or during summer. It's always best to head out as early as possible before traffic snarls end up jamming the FDR Drive or West Side Highway. The Holland Tunnel is less congested than the Lincoln Tunnel and George Washington Bridge if you're going to New Jersey. And try the Robert Kennedy Bridge rather than the Queens Midtown tunnel so you can bypass much of the congestion on your way to Long Island.

Major highways can be jammed so try for side roads or alternative routes, such as State Roads, as much as possible. The routes listed are the fastest way to your destination, but there are other, more convoluted ways to get there if traffic becomes a nightmare.

Consult your GPS if that's the case. Always give yourself more time to get to your destination and most of all, be patient and positive.

State troopers take speeding seriously, and you'll get ticketed if you don't slow down, so stick to speed limits and state laws. New York City drivers aren't the most beloved so always put your best pedal forward. Some states allow right turns on red lights, while others will fine you if you do so. Read up on any laws before heading out.

Driving to Upstate New York and to Long Island are probably the most congested routes in the book. Make sure you head out early or during a weekday to avoid traffic jams. Routes to Connecticut and the Hudson Valley are more congested in the fall, during peak foliage season. You'll get bumper-to-bumper traffic during the summer on Long Island as everyone heads east to get some sun and water time.

Construction is often a problem so check ahead to see if this will affect your trip. Beware of hills and curves on roads to smaller towns. They can get slick and wet during spring and the winter and if there is an old truss or iron bridge, driving can get even more treacherous. Drive slowly and be careful. Some of the smaller roads aren't always the best paved so beware of potholes and speed bumps. Always keep your eye on the road and your mind on safety.

public transportation

Most of the towns listed in this book can be reached by train or bus as well as car. Trains and buses are a good alternative if you're tired, part of a large party or don't want to deal with traffic jams and angry drivers. And, it's often less expensive than renting a car since it saves you the trouble of paying for gas and insurance. Many of the bigger towns have large train and bus depots at which cabs are available to take you to your destination. Most trains allow you to bring bikes onboard. Check with the particular agencies for more information.

This book lists driving routes as well as train and bus information, where applicable. Contact the following agencies to get schedules and fare information.

Amtrak
(800) 872-7245
www.amtrak.com

MTA Long Island Railroad
(718) 330-1234
www.mta.info/lirr
All trains run in and out of Penn Station, 34th Street between 7th and 8th Avenues to points in Long Island (and Queens). With ten lines (Babylon, Far Rockaway, Hempstead, Long Beach, Montauk, Oyster Bay, Port Jefferson, Port Washington, Ronkonkoma, and West Hempstead) you can get to almost anywhere you want to go from here. There is bus service available as well.

area codes

You'll be outside of the 212, 718, 646, 347, and 929 area codes. All calls require dialing 1 before the area code and then the seven-digit number.

Some area codes that you will encounter are:

914: Westchester County in New York

845: Rockland, Dutchess, Ulster, and Orange County in New York

609: central and southeastern New Jersey

908: northern New Jersey (Hunterdon and Union Counties)

215: Philadelphia and its environs

856: Burlington County in New Jersey

631: Suffolk County in Long Island, New York

610: Delaware Valley in Pennsylvania

201: Hudson and Bergen counties, as well as parts of Essex and Passaic counties in New Jersey

203: southwestern Connecticut

570: northeastern Pennsylvania

860: eastern and northwestern Connecticut

MTA Metro-North Railroad
(212) 532-4900
www.mta.info/mnr
Metro-North's five lines (New Haven, Harlem, Hudson, Pascack Valley, and Port Jervis) service points North and East of the City in New York State and Connecticut. Trains run in and out of the city from **Grand Central Station** (www.grandcentralterminal.com) and some stop at Harlem 125th Street station as well (check schedules carefully).

New Jersey Transit
(973) 275-5555
www.njtransit.com
New Jersey Transit's eight lines (Northeast Corridor, North Jersey Coast, Raritan Valley, Morris & Essex, Main/Bergen/Port Jervis, Montclair-Boonton, Pascack Valley, and Atlantic City) service points throughout New Jersey from Penn Station. NJT also has light rail connections (Hudson-Bergen, Newark, River) to smaller towns in the southern part of the

state from specific Jersey hubs. The agency also runs bus service to many towns from the Port Authority Bus Terminal (42nd Street and 8th Avenue).

highway designations

Interstates are prefaced by "I-" and are generally multilane divided highways (for example, I-95). US highways are two- and three-lane undivided roads and prefaced by US (for instance US 9). State highways/roads are paved and divided, and are prefaced by, for the sake of clarity, the respective state's abbreviation (for example, NY 32, NJ 3W). County roads can be paved or gravel and are prefaced by CR (for instance, CR 561).

where to get more information

Day trips attempt to cover a variety of bases and interests, but those looking for additional material can contact the following agencies by phone, mail, or the web. Regarding the latter, when checking out the various destinations, be aware that online reviews may be contradictory and conflicting. Everyone's experience can be different, and the web allows for a forum for these diverse opinions. So call the place directly and be conscious of ratings such as AAA and the Better Business Bureau. Some of the areas have chain hotels and restaurants, especially the more popular and larger towns, but we have not included them in the listings in this book. Here are some general resources for more information about particular towns and areas:

Fire Island Ferries
(631) 665-3600
www.fireislandferries.com

I Love New York
www.Iloveny.com

National Register of Historic Places
www.nrhp.focus.nps.gov

New Jersey Tourism
(800) VISIT-NJ
www.visitnj.org

Red and Tan Bus Lines
(201) 263-1254
http://vectour.com/redandtan

Rockland Coaches
(201) 263-1254
www.coachusa.com/rockland

SEPTA (Southeastern Pennsylvania Transportation Authority)
(215) 580-7800
www.septa.org

Visit Connecticut
(888) CT-VISIT
www.ctvisit.com

Visit Pennsylvania
(800) VISIT-PA
www.visitpa.com

north

day trip 01

north

historic hamlets:
bedford hills, new york
katonah, new york

Most day-trippers heading upstate bypass the plethora of small towns on their way to touristy destinations such as Bear Mountain and Woodstock. That's too bad as you can have a less expensive and more relaxing and rewarding time if you take a trip to the historic hamlets of Bedford Hills and Katonah. Puritan settlers from Connecticut founded Bedford Hills in 1680 (the town was originally part of Connecticut until it was annexed in 1700). Nearby Katonah was settled more than a century later by migrants from Bedford Hills. Both hamlets have managed to retain their historic flavor despite mass migration to outlying towns. The quaint mom-and-pop shops lining main street as well as the plethora of historic buildings and beautiful parks will charm you.

bedford hills

Bedford Hills is a charming town, with locally owned shops and restaurants lining the small main street. The railroad's completion in 1847 transformed sleepy Bedford Station, which it was known as then, into a business hub. In 1910, the town changed its name to Bedford Hills. Today, it's still bustling albeit at a quieter scale. An influx of tourists in the late summer and early fall head to the town's historic sights.

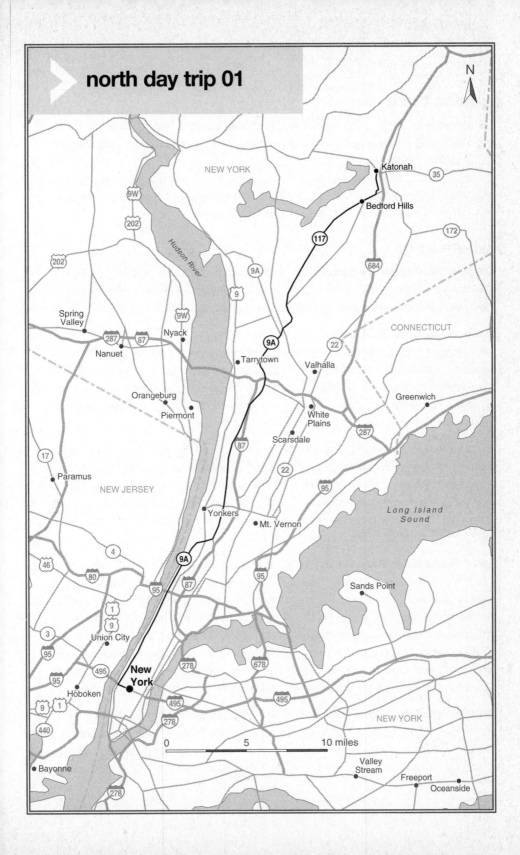

north day trip 01

getting there

Metro-North Harlem River line trains travel from Grand Central Terminal to Bedford Hills regularly throughout the day. The trip takes about an hour, past more urban suburbs such as White Plains and Scarsdale.

If you don't want to take the train to Bedford Hills, it's an easy drive from the city. Take the Henry Hudson Parkway/NY 9A to the Sawmill River Parkway N. Take the exit toward NY 117 N. Take a right at NY 117 N. It takes a little more than an hour.

where to go

Bedford Hills Historical Museum. 321 Bedford Rd., Bedford Hills; (914) 381-3356. This tiny museum houses photos of historic Bedford as well as other artifacts from the town's past. Another permanent exhibit showcases dairy farming in the area.

Bedford Museum. 615 Old Post Rd., Bedford; (914) 234-9751. Housed in the 18th-century court house, the Bedford Museum has several permanent exhibits and hosts lectures as well as mock trials for guests. Historic portraits are housed on the ground floor. The second floor houses town artifacts, dating back to its inception. Period costumes and other textiles are often on display as well as objects used by early settlers. The oldest jail cell in Westchester County can be found on the second floor.

Bedford School House. 11 Pound Ridge Rd.; (914) 234-9751. Built in 1829, this stone building, located on the village green in the nearby hamlet of Bedford (Bedford, Bedford Hills, and Katonah are all in the same jurisdiction), served as a schoolhouse for almost 100 years. The building was restored in the mid-2000s as the foundation had deteriorated somewhat. Desks date back 100 years and the Bedford Historical Society hopes to introduce other furniture used at the building's birth. Guests learn about the school's history.

Ward Pound Ridge Reservation. NY 35 and NY 121 South, Pound Ridge; (914) 864-7317. If you have a car, head to this 4,300-acre park, the largest in the county. Miles of hiking trails abound. The parks department hosts horticulture classes as well as other activities during the warmer months. Bring your lunch and picnic at a number of areas in the massive nature preserve. Camp at lean-tos and ski during the winter months. Head to the Trailside Nature Museum, established in 1937, to view Native American artifacts and listen to specialty lectures on the weekends. Children will find some of the programs particularly educational. The Gallery in the Park exhibits a variety of local art throughout the year.

Westmoreland Sanctuary. 260 Chestnut Ridge Rd., Bedford Corners; (914) 666-8448. Take I-684 S from Bedford Hills to this 640-acre wildlife refuge in Bedford Corners. It's amazing to see how such a deeply wooded area can exist in a densely populated suburban area. Learn about native birds, insects, forestry, and cider making, among other activities, throughout the year. Fall and winter are especially exciting because of hawk-watching excursions. It's an inexpensive way to spend the day.

where to shop

Bedford Sportsman. 5 Adams St., Bedford Hills; (914) 666-8091. This fishing and tackle shop has been serving the community for more than 40 years. If you're an angler looking for gear, this is the place to go. Most of the equipment is top of the line, and the prices are pretty affordable. The shop also hosts fly-tying classes as well as fishing charters to nearby rivers and lakes.

Preppy Turtle. 2 Depot Plaza, Suite 101B, Bedford Hills; (914) 666-8500. Most consignment shops are geared toward adult women but the Preppy Turtle offers designer clothing for children and teens (as well as children's toys, cribs, and other accessories at The Turtle's Nest). Owner Kathleen Luparello only stocks items from current seasons, and the selection changes fairly often.

R.D. Carone and Company. 380 Adams St., Bedford Hills; (914) 231-1172. If you're looking to restore a family heirloom or a priceless antique, head to R.D. Carone and Company. The shop has refinished furniture for more than 30 years. Owner Richard Carone is a lifelong craftsman who has done everything from veneer repair to French polishing to parts duplication. Carone and his staff are friendly and happy to sit down and chat with visitors.

where to eat

The Perennial Chef. 25 Depot Plaza, Bedford Hills; (914) 666-6523. Korean-born chef Michael serves an ever-changing menu of American classics, Mediterranean standbys, and Asian mainstays. It's kind of a hodge podge of dishes but somehow it works beautifully. A wide range of sides caters to every palate. $$.

Table Local Market. 11 Babbitt Rd., Bedford Hills; (914) 241-0269. Martha Stewart and chef Jean-Georges Vongerichten are huge fans of this LEED-certified market and restaurant near the Bedford Hills train station. Table sells and serves farm-fresh organic produce, locally raised meats, and other artisanal goods. Most visitors come here to shop and end up staying for lunch. The organic fair-trade coffee is reasonably priced and packs a flavor wallop. The menu changes fairly regularly but you can't go wrong with a mozzarella and tomato sandwich or an Amish cheddar grilled cheese. $$$.

katonah

Head to the train station and take the next Metro-North training heading to Southeast (which is not a direction but the name of a town). Katonah is a bit more developed and lively than

Bedford Hills. The streets are still small and charming, with a plethora of mom-and-pop shops and galleries. Residents are inordinately proud of their town. A century ago, they moved 55 buildings in the town to higher ground rather than see them destroyed by the construction of the Croton Dam.

getting there

Katonah is just one stop further north on Metro-North. It's about four minutes from Bedford Hills by train. Avoid traveling during peak rush hour times as trains are packed with commuters. Weekends are always the best bet. If you have a car, it's a short drive from Bedford Hills to Katonah. Take Adams Street north towards Harris Road. Take a left on Harris Road and a right on Bedford Road. At the fork, take a right onto Katonah Avenue. It's about a 7-minute drive.

where to go

Caramoor Center for Music and the Arts. 149 Girdle Ridge Rd., Katonah; (914) 232-1252. If you drove by this Mediterranean-style mansion you'd think it was a private residence. Well, it was once. Walter and Lucie Rosen bought the 100-acre estate in 1928, built the villa over the course of 10 years, and began hosting musical evenings for family and friends. After their son died in World War II, the Rosens transformed the estate from a home to a center for music and the arts. Since 1945, Caramoor has entertained the public with exceptional talent from the opera, classical, and jazz sphere including Yo-Yo Ma. Most of the talent performs in the open-air Spanish Courtyard or the indoor Venetian Theater, the latter of which was built after the Rosens' death in 1958. The estate hosts tours of the home and museum. Guests can picnic in the Italianate gardens prior to the International Music Festival, which is held during the summer every year.

John Jay Homestead State Historic Site. 400 Jay St., Katonah; (914) 232-8119. Visitors interested in early American history will particularly delight in a visit to John Jay Homestead. Once the home of John Jay, a founding father and the first Chief Justice of the Supreme Court, the 62-acre home and farm has been welcoming history buffs since 1964. Guided tours take you through 12 lovingly restored period rooms in the main home (the house has 24 rooms in all), built in 1801, as well as the 19th-century schoolhouse and barn on the grounds. Guests can picnic on the grounds throughout the year, and dogs on a leash are welcome. The homestead also hosts gallery exhibitions and lectures by noted historians throughout the year.

Katonah Museum of Art. 134 Jay St., Katonah; (914) 232-9555. This 10,000-square-foot contemporary arts museum is one of the most renowned in the country. The KMA hosts numerous art exhibitions, workshops, lectures, and outdoor concerts throughout the year. It's also part of the Fairfield/Westchester County Museum Alliance, which fosters arts education throughout two counties in New York and Connecticut. The sculpture exhibits are particularly fascinating and are held in both the South Lawn and the tranquil Sculpture Garden. The Learning Center offers workshops for children 3 and older.

where to shop

Katonah General Store. 109 Katonah Ave., Katonah; (914) 232-6400. This vintage-feeling store doesn't have sundry items, as the same would suggest. Instead, it boasts a good selection of one-of-a-kind women's clothing, jewelry, shoes, handbags, and other items. Owner June Goldfinger lovingly displays items to their best advantage. Items can be a bit pricey but are worth the splurge.

Noka. 25 Katonah Ave., Katonah; (914) 232-7278. Noka boasts an eclectic selection of vintage furniture, toys, and other knickknacks. Head to the second floor to browse through a selection of colorful and funky furniture. The coffee table selection is quite extensive although prices are a bit on the high side. The main floor houses the adult and children's gifts sections, much of which is unique or retro-inspired. Stay for a cup of coffee. The ground floor doubles as a coffee shop.

Tall Couture. 51 Bedford Rd., Suite 8, Katonah; (914) 232-1390. If you're a woman and over 5' 8" tall, you probably have a hard time finding clothing that fits your frame. Enter Tall Couture, which provides a wealth of items, from dresses to pants to outwear, specifically made for statuesque women. Pant inseams start at 36-inches, 4 more than the average. The designer jeans selection is quite extensive for the market. The shop also runs a large Internet mail-order business if you are too busy to shop but like the items for sale.

where to eat

Blue Dolphin Ristorante. 175 Katonah Ave., Katonah; (914) 232-4791. Housed in a vintage diner, the Blue Dolphin serves authentic Italian fare with a twist. Only the freshest, seasonal ingredients are used (the pasta and desserts are all made on the premises). Locals head here for the veal ravioli with ham in a tomato cream sauce as well as the delectable chicken marsala. Come on a Wednesday night when the chef cooks up some innovative specials from his birthplace of Capri. No reservations required. $$.

Katonah Restaurant. 63 Katonah Ave., Katonah; (914) 232-9241. An upscale diner not far from the train station. The decor is elegant. Tiffany-style lamps hang from the ceiling and most seats have a outdoor view. Head here for a quick bite. Traditional diner fare is interspersed with homey Greek dishes. Most of the dishes are good, especially the eggs. During summer months, you can dine al fresco. $$.

where to stay

Bedford Post. 954 Old Post Rd., Bedford; (914) 234-7800. Neither Bedford Hills nor Katonah offer lodgings but nearby Bedford, the third of the historic hamlets in the area, does. The Bedford Post, owned by actor Richard Gere and his wife Carey Lowell, boasts an 8-room inn (as well as 2 restaurants). Rooms are exquisitely appointed with Frette linens and towels, working fireplaces, brocade bolster pillows, and expansive Carerra marble baths with imported claw-foot tubs. Guests can take part in a complimentary yoga class and dine on homemade baked goods each morning. Weekend guests enjoy a free wine-and-cheese happy hour. $$$.

day trip 02

north

>>>

arts & antiques:
cold spring, new york
beacon, new york

Antiquing is a favorite pastime for many a day-tripper, and a visit to the towns of Cold Spring and Beacon doesn't disappoint. These arts and antiques hubs are about 50 to 60 miles north of New York City. Cold Spring is home to a multitude of antiques shops, offering pre-war and 19th-century finds. Beacon, further north, is an epicenter for the arts. Not that long ago, main street was run down and many historic storefronts had been boarded up. Thanks to the art museum Dia:Beacon, these abandoned shops have been converted into galleries, restaurants, and even a glassblowing studio.

cold spring

A plethora of picturesque tree-lined streets. A river's-edge park and promenade that lets you relax peacefully while admiring the mighty Hudson. A charming downtown that is clean and teeming with life. That's Cold Spring. You could spend hours meandering from one antiques shop to another. If you get tired of shopping, rent a kayak and head to the Hudson, which is a block from main street. On a summer's day, it doesn't get better than quietly paddling up the placid Hudson, past scenic mountains. The village boasts a burgeoning arts and music scene, thanks to an influx of city dwellers who now call it home.

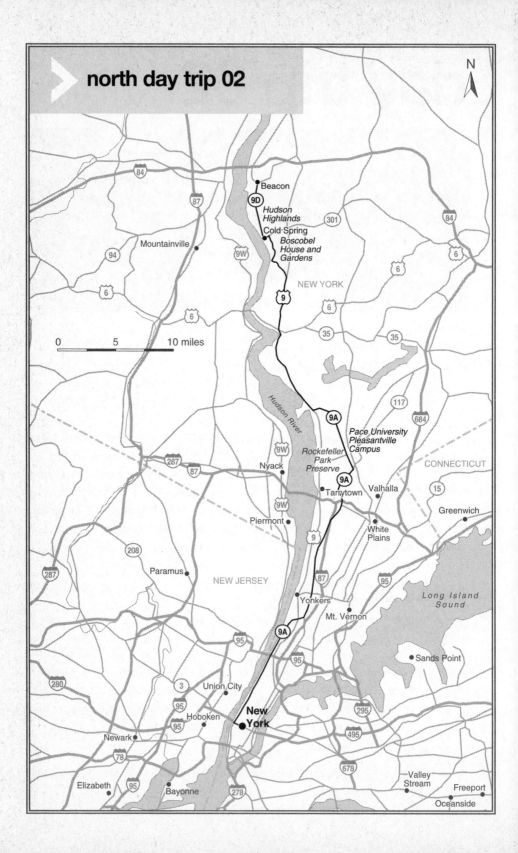

north day trip 02

getting there

Metro-North Harlem River line trains travel from Grand Central Terminal to Cold Spring hourly throughout the day. The trip takes about an hour and 10 minutes. If you'd rather take a car, it's an easy drive north. From Manhattan, take the Henry Hudson Parkway to the Sawmill River Parkway N. Connect to the Taconic State Parkway towards Albany. Exit onto NY 9A/Sawmill River Road. Keep left (the Sawmill River Road becomes Briarcliff-Peekskill Parkway). Merge onto NY 9A/US 9 N. Take a left onto NY 403 N. Turn right at NY 9D/Bear Mountain-Beacon Parkway. The trip takes a little less than a half an hour, without traffic.

where to go

Boscobel House and Gardens. 1601 NY 9D, Garrison; (845) 265-3638. Just a short trolley ride from Cold Spring lies the Peter and Elizabeth Dyckman estate in Garrison. Boscobel House is situated on the banks of the Hudson and offers a remarkable view of the river and beyond. The home is a breathtaking example of Federal architecture. Guided tours take guests inside the house, built in 1808 (some of the tours are conducted in costume), through the entry hall, up the curving staircase to Elizabeth Dyckman's bedroom, and beyond. Once back outside, visitors are encouraged to take a turn around the rose gardens, springhouse, and orangery. The museum collection and exhibits include historic documents as well as vintage paintings, clocks, and furniture. Summer concerts are often held on the grounds.

Putnam County Historical Society & Foundry School Museum. 63 Chestnut St., Cold Spring; (845) 265-4010. Founded in 1906, The Putnam County Historical Society operates the Foundry School Museum, which educated children of West Point Foundry workers as well as its apprentices during the 19th century. The organization preserves historic documents and artifacts related to the West Point Foundry and Putnam County. Exhibits range from historic postcards to vintage photos of the Hudson Highlands to Native American paraphernalia to Gilded Age fashion trends.

West Point Foundry Preserve Cold Spring. This 87-acre preserve was once home to the West Point Foundry. Today, it's an archaeological site. Besides the miles of scenic trails, visitors can meander through the remains of the iron works operation, which functioned from the early- to late-1800s. Workers at the foundry built the Parrott Gun, a rifled cannon that was instrumental in helping the Union win the Civil War. Many of the brick foundry buildings remain, but are in disrepair. The foundry's office building is the only one that still has a roof.

where to shop

Cold Spring Antiques Center. 77 Main St., Cold Spring; (845) 265-5050. This 2,000-square-foot space, housed in a Victorian bank, boasts antiques and other vintage items from 25 local dealers. Choose from a wide array of furniture, paintings, jewelry, and clothing, some of which are on display in the vintage bank vault. Prices run the gamut from as little as $1 to $3,000. The center, which has been operating since 2003, is open year-around except for Thanksgiving and Christmas. Free to the pubic. Closed Tues and Wed.

Cold Spring Train Works. 165 Main St.; (845) 265-2906. Locomotive junkies and the kids who love them could spend hours at this expansive store. Cold Spring Train Works carries 4,000 different items relating to trains, including full model sets, rolling stock, scenery supplies, wooden trains, and tracks. Brands include Thomas the Tank Engine, Athearn, Atlas, and Walthers. New customers receive a discount on their initial purchase.

Hudson Valley Outfitters. 63 Main St., Cold Spring; (845) 265-0221. Although Cold Spring is an antiques mecca, many visitors head here for outdoor activities. Hudson Valley Outfitters is the town's preeminent sporting gear supplier. The shop is only a block from the train station. Stop here if you want to rent or buy a kayak for a ride up river. Kayaks are available for 1-, 2-, and 4-hour rides. The store also runs guided tours of the river as well as kayak instruction classes from May through October.

where to eat

Foundry Cafe. 55 Main St., Cold Spring; (845) 265-4504. A small and homey eatery, the Foundry Cafe is a local favorite mainly due to its extensive coffee selection and breakfast items but also for its vegetarian sandwiches and homemade quiche. The trendy spot is bustling in the summer when outdoor seats are available. Daily specials are posted on the chalkboard wall behind the checkout counter. $$.

Riverview. 45 Fair St., Cold Spring; (845) 265-4778. Just a short distance from Main Street, lies this contemporary American eatery that gets accolades not only for its market-fresh food but also for its majestic views of the Hudson River and nearby Storm King Mountain. Local artwork hangs on blue walls and service is attentive. The brick oven pizza is oozing with flavor, and the veal is particularly tender. Finish your meal with a key lime tart. $$.

where to stay

Hudson House River Inn. 2 Main St., Cold Spring; (845) 265-9355. The Hudson House River Inn was built in 1832 on the waterfront of Cold Spring. That strategic location affords guests picturesque views of West Point and Storm King mountain. This restored historic building is as lovely on the inside as it is on the outside. Guests can choose from 13 cozy rooms and suites, each impeccably furnished with antiques and brass beds. Rooms have their own private bathrooms featuring Crabtree and Evelyn products. Standard rooms overlook the main street not the water so upgrade to a river view room to get the full benefit of staying here. Discounts apply during the off-season, when the Hudson House offers staycation packages for couples. $$$.

Kittleman House. 45 Main St., Cold Spring; (845) 265-3697. Kittleman House is a truly inviting place with great attentive service. Kathleen and Jim Kittleman run a beautiful yet unpretentious home. The decor is homey yet elegant. Rooms are surprisingly spacious, with four-poster beds, antiques, and hardwood floors. Jim cooks a mean breakfast, and Kathleen ensures that guests' needs are met, surprising them with personal touches and gifts. $$.

beacon

Beacon is aptly named. An epicenter for contemporary art, the tree-lined main street features a number of historic buildings that have been transformed into galleries. Artists rent space in town and create contemporary masterpieces. The town hosts a citywide celebration on the second Saturday of every month throughout the year. Galleries and shops host musical and arts events into the late evening. Storefront windows display art installations during the monthlong Windows on Main Street festival in August. The town gets tourists throughout the year thanks to amazing exhibits at Dia:Beacon.

getting there

Take Metro-North two stops north from Cold Spring to Beacon. It's about 10 to 15 minutes from Cold Spring by train. Avoid traveling during peak rush hour times as trains are packed with commuters. Weekends are always the best bet. Beacon is a short, 11-minute drive from Cold Spring. Take NY 9D N to Teller Avenue. Take a right on Teller and a left on Henry Street to the center of town.

where to go

Dia:Beacon. 3 Beekman St., Beacon; (845) 440-0100. A short walk up the hill from the train station leads you to this 240,000-square-foot museum of contemporary art, the largest of its kind in the country. The permanent exhibits, which feature works by Andy Warhol, Gerard Richter, and Louise Bourgeois, among others, hold visitors in thrall. The sculptures bring calm and peace. Sol Lewitt's Drawing Series is particularly fascinating. Two full teams of drafters executed the work, which occupies several rooms in the main gallery. On the more experimental side, a "work as action" exhibition requires viewers/participants to unfold pieces of canvas, play with them, and fold them back up. Free guided tours run on Saturday afternoons throughout the year.

Madam Brett Homestead Museum. 50 Van Nydeck Ave., Beacon; (845) 831-6533. This is the oldest home in Dutchess County and was used to shelter patriots and store military supplies during the Revolutionary War. Built in 1709, the home housed seven generations of the Brett/Teller family. It became a museum in 1954. Visitors can tour 17 rooms with original period furnishings as well as the five-acre grounds with a brook and a garden.

> ## museums of modern art

*It's something of a surprise to many New Yorkers to find that Beacon, New York, offers a wealth of terrific art galleries and art studios, showcasing talented emerging and unknown artists. While we have the MOMA, Beacon has **Dia:Beacon,** one of the most brilliant contemporary art museums in the country. Some people claim that the museum single-handedly saved the town from economic ruin as much of the downtown area was boarded up or vacated. Now art lovers can head to Dia:Beacon as well as a number of other galleries including **Beahive/ Antidote Collective** (291 Main St., Suite No. 1; 917-449-6356; www.beahive beacon.com), a community workspace; **Beacon Studios** (211 Fishkill Ave.; www .beaconstudios.org), a creative space in the old Beacon High School; and **Beacon Artist Union** (161 Main St.; 845-440-7548; www.beaconartistunion.com), a collective featuring figurative, abstract, and 4-dimensional works.*

Mount Beacon Incline Railway. Mount Beacon, Beacon; (845) 765-3262. The ruins of this funicular are quite a sight to see. Built in 1902, the railway carried thousands of passengers more than 2,000 feet to the summit of Mount Beacon . . . and back. A fire destroyed the operation in the mid-1980s. Guided tours take visitors up a scenic trail to the railway's ruins, which is on the National Register of Historic Places. The group behind the restoration hopes to one day have it operating again.

Mount Gulian Historic Site. 145 Sterling St., Beacon; (845) 831-8172. Nestled on 44 acres, this 18th-century Dutch estate was home to settler Abraham Isaac Verplanck and his family. Verplanck transferred use of his home to General Friedrich von Steuben and the Continental Army in 1782. Tours take you through the restored 1740s barn as well as the 19th-century rose gardens. The site also hosts reenactment-style dinners and auctions.

where to shop

Alps Sweet Shop. 269 Main St., Beacon; (845) 831-8240. Since 1922, this Hudson Valley chocolatier has been creating homemade sweets to area residents. Boxed chocolates are lovingly made. The "Signal Fire Toffee" is a local favorite. Choose from an array of more than 100 different items.

Hudson Beach Glass. 162 Main St., Beacon; (845) 440-0068. Opened in 2003 in a restored 1890s firehouse, this glass studio and gallery sells exquisite handblown glass bowls, vases, candelabras, perfume bottles, and sculptures at reasonable prices. You can watch glass-blowers at work and even take glass-making classes. The second floor gallery doubles as an event space. Throughout the year, Hudson Beach hosts wine and beer tastings.

Riverwinds Gallery. 172 Main St., Beacon; (845) 838-2880. If you're looking for landscapes, architectural drawings, and watercolors by Hudson Valley artists, look no further than Riverwinds Gallery. Much of the work depicts bucolic scenes. Local artists on display include Peter Billman, Allison Cross, and Virginia Donovan. The gallery also showcases home decor, ceramics, and jewelry.

where to eat

Beacon Fall's Cafe. 472 Main St., Beacon; (845) 765-0172. Beacon Falls Cafe serves American fare in a cozy, casual setting. Owner Brad Nevelus is a Culinary Institute of America grad and it shows in his delectable dishes. A BLT salmon panini, sweet potato fries, and artisan salad are three lunch highlights. Much of the wine and beer is local. Prices are fairly affordable for being in a popular part of town. $$.

Chill Wine Bar. 173 Main St.; (845) 765-0885. City dwellers will find themselves at home at this wine bar. Exposed brick and leather chairs dot the cozy space. Although Chill serves small plates, head here for an extensive array of quality wine and beer, much of it from the Hudson Valley and Finger Lakes. Saturday night features live jazz. $$.

Homespun Foods. 232 Main St.; (845) 831-5096. A Zagat's favorite, this casual cafe serves fresh, locally-sourced, seasonal fare with a smile. Sandwiches and salads are the specialty. During the fall, head here for delicious butternut squash and apple soup and vegetarian meatloaf. The desserts are particularly delicious, especially the cookies and tarts. A patio garden operates in warm weather months. The cafe also runs an artisanal market. $$.

where to stay

Botsford Briar Bed-and-Breakfast. 19 High St., Beacon; (845) 831-6099. This lovely Victorian bed-and-breakfast is just a stone's throw away from the Metro-North Station and Dia:Beacon. Situated on a hill overlooking the historic district, Botsford Briar Bed-and-Breakfast is less than 30 years old but the structure dates back to the late 19th century. Proprietors Shirley Botsford and Charles Fincham make you feel right at home. Rooms are lovingly decorated without the kitsch found in most bed-and-breakfasts. All have queen beds, restored antiques, elegant color schemes, and drapery and private baths. The Magnolia Room is the best of the bunch as it has a Florida room (enclosed porch) affording views of the majestic Hudson. $$$.

Mt. Beacon Bed-and-Breakfast. 829 Wolcott Ave.; (845) 831-0737. There are several lodging options in Beacon but Mt. Beacon Bed-and-Breakfast is the best of the lot. The accommodations are elegantly appointed, with high ceilings, Victorian antiques, and polished hardwood floors. The nautical-themed Captain's Stateroom is the most charming of the three rooms. Guests have use of the terracotta patio and in-ground pool. $$.

day trip 03

north

>>> **spooky new york:**
tarrytown, new york
sleepy hollow, new york

If you're a spooky little girl like me, you love haunted houses, ghost stories, and visiting towns known for their otherworldly residents. The legendary towns of Tarrytown and Sleepy Hollow have a well-deserved ghostly reputation; traveling through town on a cold winter's night can conjure up images of headless horsemen and lamenting women in white. Tarrytown is the more famous of the two, having been the residence of writer Washington Irving. Sleepy Hollow needs no introduction to fans of American literature. Both towns are popular destinations during Halloween but you can head here anytime of year to experience ghostly enchantment.

tarrytown

Tarrytown has it all: history, dining, shopping, and nature. The town sits on a bluff overlooking the Hudson River, and many shops and restaurants afford great views. The town is best known as the residence of Washington Irving, author of *The Legend of Sleepy Hollow*. Many of the town's buildings date back to the 19th century, when it was a sleepy hamlet and farming community. Today, the town sees an influx of tourists during the fall when ghostly happenings are commemorated. The ruins of the Graystone and Pinkstone estates are especially spooky if you'd like to get off the beaten track.

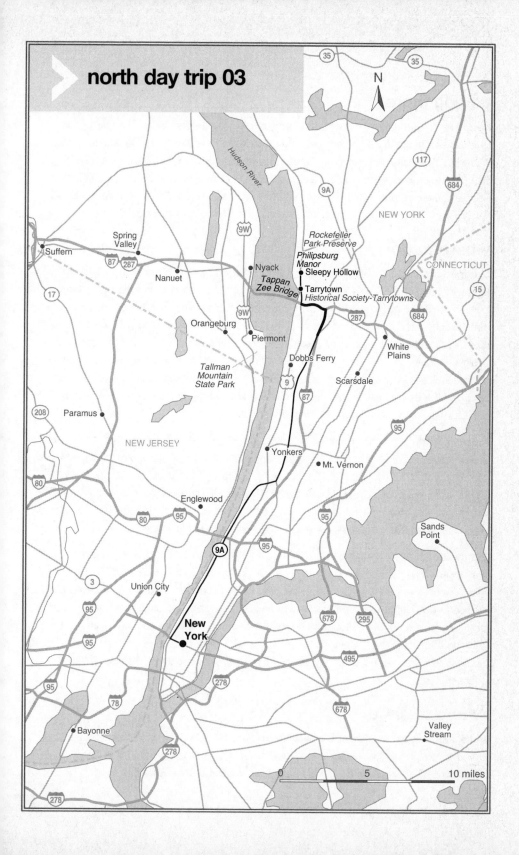

getting there

Metro-North has regular service via the Hudson River line to Tarrytown. The ride to Tarrytown varies. On some trains, you can get there in less than 40 minutes. On others, it takes nearly 50. The center of town is not far from the station. Just an hour drive from New York City, Tarrytown is easy to get to. Take the Henry Hudson Parkway to the Saw Mill River Parkway N. Merge onto I-87 N via the ramp to I-287/Tappan Zee Bridge. Take exit 9 to US 9/Tarrytown. Take a left on White Plains Road and a right on South Broadway.

where to go

Lyndhurst. 635 South Broadway, Tarrytown; (914) 631-4481. A National Historic Trust Site, Lyndhurst is a 67-acre estate on the banks of the Hudson. Designed by Alexander Davis in 1838, the gothic revival mansion was once ridiculed by townsfolk for its noncolonial, romantic style. The estate was home to several famous Americans, including railroad magnate Jay Gould, who bought it as a summer home in the late 1800s. The interiors feature original works by Tiffany, Bourguereau, and Daubigny, and the sweeping grounds feature evergreens, a rose garden, and greenhouse fernery. The vestibule is particularly awe-inspiring. The estate hosts horticulture and jazz events throughout the spring and summer. A LEGO weekend in April draws children from miles around.

Patriot's Park. 121 North Broadway, Tarrytown; (914) 631-8347. Situated on the border of Tarrytown and Sleepy Hollow, Patriot's Park is famous for Captor's Monument, which commemorates the capture of British spy John André by Revolutionary War heroes John Paulding, Isaac Van Wart, and David Williams. The three Tarrytown militiamen caught André with traitor Benedict Arnold's plans to sell out West Point stashed in his boot. The park also plays host to a farmers' market every Saturday from June to November.

Sunnyside. 89 West Sunnyside Lane, Tarrytown; (914) 591-8763. Sunnyside was home to Washington Irving, America's first internationally acclaimed author. Built in 1835, the main house was expanded through the years. The colonial cottage, covered in wisteria, has amazing views of the Hudson River as well as luxurious gardens. Guides, in period dress, lead guests on a 45-minute tour of the grounds and home. Guests can also picnic on the grounds after their tour. In late October, Sunnyside hosts a Legend Celebration, which incorporates *The Legend of Sleepy Hollow* puppet shows, spooky walks, live music, and ghost stories.

where to shop

Bella's Boutique. 35 North Broadway, Tarrytown; (914) 333-7778. An exotic and cozy shop filled to the gills with locally made artisanal items as well as imported finds. The jewelry selection is quite extensive but it's the handbag selection that truly delights.

The Weaving Center of Tarrytown. 32 Warren Ave., Tarrytown; (914) 332-1948. Sister Bianca Haglich runs this weaving center housed in Marymount Convent's old gym. Haglich teaches group workshops as well as private one-on-one. Looms are for rent. The nonprofit center also sells shawls, scarves, and blankets throughout the year, but has a bigger selection during the holiday season.

Whimsies Incognito. 35 South Broadway, Tarrytown; (914) 631-3355. Housed in a historic building, Whimsies boasts an interesting array of handcrafted, artisanal gifts, specifically jewelry, scarves, cards, frames, and ornaments. Owner Jackie Golabek hosts sales throughout the year, so check back often. The skeleton key selection is particularly extensive.

where to eat

Blue Hill at Stone Barns. 630 Bedford Rd., Tarrytown; (914) 366-9600. Like its outpost in lower Manhattan, Blue Hill serves fresh, locally-sourced cuisine, much of which comes from the nearby Stone Barns Center for Food and Agriculture. Blue Hill concocts customized menus featuring seasonal items such as African geese, Alcosa cabbage, and Orion fennel. Lunch is more affordable than dinner, but the 8-course Farmer's Feast is worth the splurge since many of the items can't be found elsewhere. $$$.

Lefteris Gyro. 1 Main St., Tarrytown; (914) 524-9687. Housed in a Tudor-style building in the center of town, this cozy Greek restaurant is always packed with budget-minded diners looking for good food. The gyros and moussaka are some of the best in the New York City area. $.

where to stay

Castle on the Hudson. 400 Benedict Ave., Tarrytown; (914) 631-1980. Built by the son of a Civil War general, this medieval-style hotel has served as a private home, boarding school for boys, and an investment business. Today, it sits on manicured lawns and boasts 31 luxurious rooms and suites with views of the river, woodburning fireplaces, four-poster canopied beds, marble baths, and goose down comforters. Opt for the turret rooms if you can as the views are truly majestic. Equus restaurant is a Zagat favorite for its hearty American fare. $$.

Tarrytown House Estate. 49 East Sunnyside Lane, Tarrytown; (800) 553-8118. This expansive hotel sits on 26 meticulously landscaped acres just minutes from downtown Tarrytown and Washington Irving's Sunnyside estate. The lodging occupies two buildings—the main house and the King Mansion. The main building has 212 rooms decorated in clean, modern lines and with all the amenities, including carpeted floors, complimentary Wi-Fi, Nintendo, interactive TV entertainment, and large baths with relaxing showers. The King Mansion is where you want to be if you want more luxury and privacy. The 10 rooms are situated in a 19th-century Georgian manse and come with large four-poster beds, hardwood floors, oriental rugs, and windows overlooking the green lawn. $$$.

sleepy hollow

It's been said that Washington Irving's tale of haunted horsemen and death was based on local legends stemming back to the Native Americans, and most of the area described in *The Legend of Sleepy Hollow* is relatively unchanged from that time with a lot of it contained in Rockefeller Park Preserve. Sleepy Hollow has a spookier vibe than Tarrytown, due in part to the tale as well as to the eerie Sleepy Hollow Cemetery, the final resting place of more than 35,000 former residents, including Revolutionary War soldiers and Irving himself.

getting there

Take the Metro-North one stop north to Philipse Manor, which is the stop in Sleepy Hollow. It's about five to 10 minutes from Tarrytown. If you have a car take North Broadway from Tarrytown until you reach Sleepy Hollow. It's about a 5-minute drive.

where to go

Kykuit. 200 Lake Rd., Pocantico Hills; (914) 631-9491. Situated on hundreds of acres, the 100-year-old former Rockefeller estate is an art and architecture lover's paradise. A 6-story, 40-room Georgian home should be the starting point. Take the 3-hour Grand Tour as you will get to see the expansive second floor with priceless works of 20th-century art and antiques. The sweeping, manicured Beaux-Arts gardens feature an awe-inspiring collection of 20th-century sculpture. Subterranean art galleries include Picasso tapestries and works by Chagall and Warhol, and the 3-story Coach Barn has a collection of vintage carriages and classic cars.

Phillipsburg Manor. 381 North Broadway, Sleepy Hollow; (914) 631-3992. The wealthy Dutch Philipse family, who owned 90,000 acres of Westchester before the Revolution (and lost it all after backing the wrong side), built this 17th-century farm. Today, it has been lovingly restored with actors recreating much of what life was like on the estate for staff and slaves. The 300-year-old manor home features period furnishings and reproductions. Tour the working gristmill and the Dutch barn, both of which feature demonstrations of colonial life.

Rockefeller State Park Preserve. Sleepy Hollow. A gift from the Rockefeller family, who still own 3,000 neighboring acres, this expansive playground offers miles of scenic trails and peaceful spots at which to rest. Yet, it has an eerie vibe. Maybe it's the mind playing tricks, but many hikers have felt a strange presence while meandering through Witches Spring Trail and Spook Rock Trail. Legend has it that in colonial days there was a woman who lived in those woods as an herbalist and healer. Threatened local leaders—men, *natch*—accused her of being a witch and had her driven out of town.

where to shop

Hennessy Home Accents. 16 New Broadway, Sleepy Hollow; (914) 631-2068. Housed in a Victorian home, this cute shop sells vintage and new furniture such as accent tables, trunks, and primitive pieces from Kentucky. Local artists are showcased at the store's third-floor gallery.

where to eat

Bridge View Tavern. 226 Beekman Ave., Sleepy Hollow; (914) 332-0078. This homey pub has a 44-seat dining room affording views of the Tappan Zee Bridge, a plethora of flat screen TVs and a rock-centric jukebox. The menu skews toward smoky meats. Get the brisket. A good number of craft beers are on tap, several of which are local. $$.

The Horseman Restaurant and Pizza. 276 North Broadway, Sleepy Hollow; (914) 631-2984. This cozy 20-year-old restaurant has a diner feel and is very family friendly. It's open for breakfast, lunch, and dinner but breakfast is the best option. The Horseman makes the best pancakes in town and its corn beef hash can't be beat. $$.

worth more time

The Union Church (555 Bedford Rd., Pocantico Hills) is worth a side trip. The stone church, built in the 1920s, was—you guessed it—the Rockefeller family church. It features nearly a dozen stained glass windows by Chagall and Matisse (it was Matisse's last work before his death in 1954).

day trip 04

north

hudson valley wineries:
marlboro, new york
millbrook, new york

Wineries have run amuck in New York State but certain areas are less well known. The Finger Lakes and North Fork regions are world renowned for producing some top quality vino. But Hudson Valley isn't on many a wine drinker's radar. That's about to change as the area is aggressively pursuing tourists.

This day trip takes you to two towns in Ulster and Dutchess counties known for making quality wine in the Hudson Valley. Halfway between New York City and Albany lies the tiny 300-year-old farming hamlet of Marlboro, a spot famous for its organic produce and abundant wineries. Millbrook is a tiny village on the other side of the river that was settled by Quakers in the 1700s. Today, it's horse and hound country with wine becoming a major source of revenue and tourism.

marlboro

A farming community that was settled by European immigrants more than 300 years, Marlboro retains its bucolic origins even though it's on the upswing thanks to a growing population as well as its commitment to sustainability. Most area businesses are committed to eco-friendly practices and town inhabitants promote environmental tourism. This is where you head for fresh organic produce, fine wine, and agri-cuisine. Locals are friendly and happy to suggest particular diversions for day trippers so don't be afraid to ask.

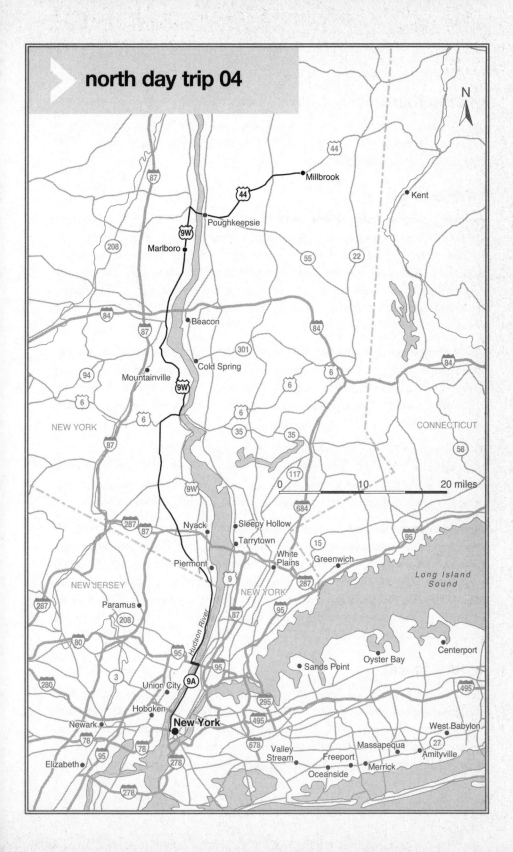

getting there

Only 70 miles from New York City, it's a gorgeous, hour and a half ride through farmland and bucolic pastures. From New York City, take the Palisades Interstate Parkway to US 6E onto US 9W north to Marlboro.

where to go

Benmarl Winery at Slate Hill Vineyards. 156 Highland Ave., Marlboro; (845) 236-4265. Called "America's oldest vineyard," Benmarl is a family-run winery that is known in the Hudson Valley for its Riesling, Baco Noir and Muscat. Wines are aged in oak or stainless steel barrels. The views from the estate are spectacular. The winery sponsors Customer Appreciation Days in which guests enjoy free tastings and discounts on wine purchases. The winery also hosts concerts and events throughout the year. The fall Stomp Festival draws crowds from miles around.

Glorie Farm Winery. 40 Mountain Rd., Marlboro; (845) 236-3265. This small family-run winery with an adjacent fruit farm is only seven years young. It overlooks the Marlborough reservoir from its Mt. Zion location. Glorie Farm produces only 600 cases of wine each year. Local favorites include Seyvel Blanc and Cabernet Franc. The winery makes personalized special label wines for weddings, birthdays, etc.

Mountain Fresh Farms. 282 Orchard Rd., Highland; (845) 795-2260. A year-round hydro-ponic farm in nearby Highland that sells a variety of fruits and vegetables to local supermar-kets and has a wealth of herbs—basil, mint, sage, etc.—available onsite. The property also boasts a Christmas Tree farm, complete with cut trees, wreaths, and wagon rides.

Stoutridge Vineyard. 10 Ann Kaley Lane, Marlboro; (845) 236-7620. Since 1902, this farm-turned-winery has had many owners. Kimberly Wagner and Stephen Osborn have owned the property since 2001. The Wagner-Osborns have restored the original outbuild-ings to their old grandeur since many of the buildings had been vandalized. The owners are committed to sustainability, so much so that they built a winemaking facility that har-nesses the power of the earth and sun to keep it running. The Pinot Noir and Sangiovese are particularly superb.

where to eat

Raccoon Saloon. 1330 US 9W, Marlboro; (845) 236-7872. An upscale restaurant unlike what the name suggests. The Raccoon Saloon serves surprisingly good food at affordable prices. Guests can watch the beautiful cascading waterfall from the back porch. Stay for a pint and a burger and fries, which have won raves from out-of-towners and locals. The Rac-coon Saloon makes its own ketchup, and the service makes you feel as if you are family. $$.

forgotten hudson valley

Up and down the Hudson Valley are places time has forgotten. There are plenty of old estates and foundries that have been lovingly restored and opened to the public, but quite a few landmarks have been left to decay. These ruins offer a diverting side trip if you're adventurous and want to see something out of the ordinary. Two of the most unique and interesting sites are the Yonkers Power Station in Yonkers and Bannerman's Island Arsenal on Pollepel Island near Beacon.

The Yonkers Power Station is visible to anyone driving up the Palisades. Built in 1906, it diligently served the area until 1971. Today, it remains abandoned save for overgrowth and rusty gauges and the odd animal sighting. Preservationists have called for it to receive landmark status, which hasn't happened as of press time.

It's truly tragic that Bannerman's Island Arsenal has been left to rot. Built over an 18-year period more than a century ago by a Scottish immigrant, it served as a warehouse complex for weaponry but was built to resemble a German castle (the Hudson River Valley was often referred to as "the American Rhine"), capturing the imagination of anyone who passed the seemingly impenetrable fortress. Abandoned by the Bannerman family in 1959, much of the arsenal was destroyed in a fire in 1969, leaving just a shell of what once stood. Hard-hat tours of the facility are available through the Bannerman Castle Trust (www.bannermancastle.org).

Ship Lantern Inn. 1725 US 9W, Milton; (845) 795-5400. This family-run restaurant is one of the oldest in all of the Hudson River Valley. It's earned accolades from Zagat, *Wine Spectator,* and other publications. The ambience is decidedly nautical with dark wood and low lighting. The Atlantic salmon and day boat scallops can't be beat. Vegetarians and children are not neglected. Both get their own specialty menus. $$.

where to stay

Buttermilk Falls Inn & Spa. 220 North Rd., Milton; (877) 746-6772. This 70-acre estate in the nearby hamlet of Milton was built in 1680. The inn was recently renovated. The 16 rooms, 3 of which are in a separate carriage house, now feature private baths, fireplaces, and high-speed Internet. Stroll through the organic gardens and follow up a long day of exercise with a treatment at the in-house geothermal spa (the spa uses organic Jurlique products). The inn even has a small fitness center. A gourmet breakfast and afternoon tea are included. $$.

millbrook

Millbrook is bucolic to the extreme. Rolling hills and open spaces abound. The area has a number of quality farm stands as well as Christmas tree farms. The small tree-lined main street is charming. Walking the length of it, you pass several antiques shops, restaurants, residences, and the public library (a newer wing has been added as an extension to the original building and was designed to mirror the same architecture).

getting there

From Marlboro take US 9W north to US 44 E onto NY 82 S. The landscape is full of rolling hills, horse farms, and beautiful estates homes. It's about 32 minutes from Marlboro, not accounting for traffic.

where to go

Millbrook Vineyards & Winery. Wing and Shunpike Roads, Millbrook; (845) 677-8383. One of the top-rated wineries in New York state, it is owned by Sonoma-based William Seylem Winery. Singer Darryl Hall of Hall & Oates fame lives in the area and is a fan of Millbrook Chardonnay. The winery creates classic French varietals such as Cabernet Franc and Pinot Noir. Guided tours take you through the winemaking process. All of the wine being poured is produced by the company, including William Seylem, Millbrook, and Italian producer Villa Pillo.

Oak Summit Vineyard. 372 Oak Summit, Millbrook; (845) 677-9522. Oak Summit is an award-wining winery. The Pinot Noir gets most of the accolades. Much of the wine is produced in the Burgundian manner. The winery offers lunch and tastings by appointment.

Orvis Sandanona Shooting Grounds. 3047 Sharon Turnpike, Millbrook; (845) 677-9701. Although Millbrook is bucolic in the extreme and most people come here for the wineries, if you've ever wanted to shoot clay pigeons, the Sandanona Shooting Grounds are the place to be. The 400-acre grounds host a 30-standing sporting clay course that is at once daunting and fun. It's considered one of the top-10 courses in the country. Long-term guests to the area can enroll in the shooting school, which teaches shooting fundamentals as well as gun safety, handling, stance, and aim. Students get to fire hundred rounds of ammo. It's a chance to let out all that aggression, and it works. The organization also hosts fly-fishing lessons.

where to shop

Citrus. 3280 Franklin St., Millbrook; (845) 677-9660. This cute shop sells women's clothing and accessories, much of it from Manhattan-based designers Josephine & Laurentina.

Seasonal sales occur throughout the year. Head here on Community Day for an additional 40 percent off.

Merritt Bookstore. 57 Front St., Millbrook; (845) 677-5857. A family-owned, independent bookstore for more than 20 years. Owner Scott Meyer sells a diverse collection of fiction and nonfiction, much of it rare or critically acclaimed. The store hosts book signings, readings, and book clubs.

where to eat

Cafe les Baux. 152 Church St., Millbrook; (845) 677-8166. This highly rated rustic French bistro is jam-packed on weekends. Chef Herve Bouchard crafts Provençal favorites such as escargot in a licorice and butter sauce and filet of sole with saffron rice and capers. The atmosphere is unpretentious, and diners are left smiling by the quality food and service. $$$.

Millbrook Cafe. 3288 Franklin Ave., Millbrook; (845) 677-6956. Millbrook Cafe, not to be confused with Millbrook Diner, is more refined than the name suggests. The owner prepares most of the food in a brick oven behind the bar, and the house specialty is 18th-century Hungarian dishes prepared in a traditional manner. The beer selection is decent and includes many European brands. Dinner is finished with a free Belgian chocolate fondue. $$.

where to stay

Cat in Your Lap. Old Route 83, Millbrook. Owners Madelyn and Bill Berensmann run this unique and cozy bed-and-breakfast. Guests have a choice of 4 accommodations, 2 in the 19th-century manse, and 2 studio apartments in the converted barn. The second option is more unique. A private patio overlooks the stream that runs through the property, and a fireplace keeps you cozy on cold winter nights. $$.

Millbrook Country House. 3244 Sharon Turnpike, Millbrook; (845) 677-9570. A lovely, intimate bed-and-breakfast that pleases the eye as well as bed-and-breakfast connoisseurs. Millbrook Country House has 4 guest rooms, named for Italian towns, design styles, and eras. Each room is elegantly appointed with period furnishings showcasing beautiful craftsmanship and attention to detail. Owners Lorraine Alexander and Giancarlo Grisi have meticulously and lovingly designed each of these rooms. No detail or flourish is without careful thought, from the ornate bed frames, to the paintings to the bowls on dressers. The Barrocco room is probably the most lavish, reflecting the Baroque period, which was known for rich colors and accents. The 18th-century Venetian bed is a sight to behold as both the headboard and footboard have been carefully carved and constructed. The hotel's grounds are some of the most beautiful at any bed-and-breakfast. Stroll through the gardens and admire the modern sculptures. $$$.

day trip 05

north

ski in, ski out:
hunter mountain, new york
windham mountain, new york
plattekill mountain, new york
belleayre mountain, new york

When New Yorkers head for the slopes, they tend to overlook nearby ski resorts. Stowe and Stratton, Vermont, take more than 4 hours to get to, but that doesn't stop snowboarders and skiers from traveling the long distance to test the powder. After all, Vermont has more ski areas than lowly New York, right? Wrong. New York has the most ski spots of any state in the nation (44 at last count). Yes, even more than Colorado or Utah. The common perception is that the slopes here are too easy. That may be true if you're Olympic caliber, but the combination of ice and cold weather make hitting the powder in New York State quite a challenge for beginning to mid-level to expert skiers. Four ski towns—Hunter, Windham, Plattekill, and Belleayre—are less than 2 hours away by car. These resorts in the Catskills offer a wealth of easy to difficult runs. Even the most experienced skier or snowboarder among you will feel challenged and invigorated after a day on the mountain.

hunter mountain

Hunter is a great mountain for a beginner. The resort has three separate mountains at which to test your balance and expertise. Most of the easy runs are located at the base of the mountain with familiar names such as Madison Park and Gramercy Park. Mid-level trails are higher up the mountain, and the dreaded black diamonds—with names such as Hell Gate

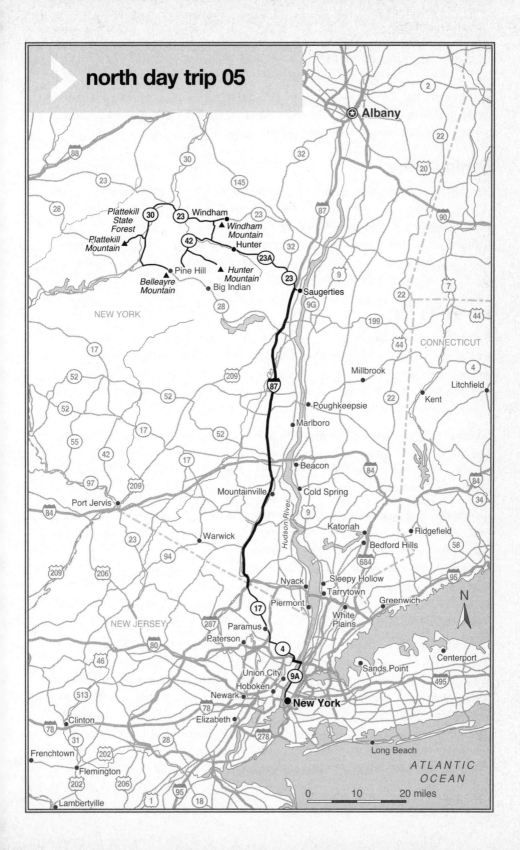

north day trip 05

and The Cliff—are clustered near the Summit Lodge. The instructors are patient and experienced but don't feel sheepish if the person teaching you is 13 years old. Snowboarders are very welcome here but you're sometimes relegated to mid-level runs.

getting there

Hunter isn't serviced by train but you can take the bus here. But it's better to rent a car with your friends and ride up on your own. Take the Lincoln Tunnel to NJ 3W. Take the NJ 17 N exit to Rutherford. Stay on NJ 17 N. It will turn into NY 17 N/I-87 N. Take exit 20 for NY 32 N to Saugerties. Continue onto NY 32A N until you see the signs for NY 23A W. Take NY 214 directly to the mountain or continue on NY 23A until you reach the town of Hunter. It's about 2 hours and 40 minutes from New York City.

where to eat

Atrium Bar at The Copper Tree. (518) 263-4223. Located at the Main Lodge, this is the spot to start your après-ski adventure. Atrium Bar at The Copper Tree Restaurant affords amazing views down the mountain. Skiers head here for craft beer, wine and signature cocktails. The Copper Tree restaurant serves classic American fare and is often the site of summertime weddings. $$.

Summit Lounge. (800) HUNTER-MTN. One of the more low-key eateries on the mountain. Accessible by chair lift from the base of the mountain to the peak. Summit Lounge serves sushi and cocktails from noon until 5 p.m. on the weekends, during the winter season only. Closed in summer. $$.

VanWinkle's Restaurant at the Kaatskill Mountain Club. (518) 263-5580. VanWinkle's Restaurant is a low-key eatery on the lift side of the mountain that's open for breakfast, lunch, dinner, après-ski, and late night cocktails. The homey atmosphere is perfect for families or anyone looking for a cozy nosh. Brick oven pizzas, burgers, and salads are the main selections on the menu. $$.

where to stay

Kaatskill Mountain Club. New Yorkers may be surprised that Hunter Mountain offers quality lodging as most Manhattanites head here for a day run. The Kaatskill Mountain Club is a rustic, ski chalet on the top of Hunter Mountain. Guests can choose from a variety of homey suites from basic studio suites featuring queen beds, sitting areas, and full baths to massive family suites with Jacuzzis, living rooms, and fully equipped kitchens. The club also plays host to several luxury condo options for large parties looking for privacy and a great views. The resort also boasts a year-round heated pool, hot tubs, fitness center, spa and steam room, and sauna. Lift and stay packages are available all season. $$$.

windham mountain

You've probably come across people who are Hunter devotees or Windham devotees. Few people venture from one to the other. Like Hunter, Windham has a reputation as a great place for beginners or rusty skiers to test the powder. Windham is probably just a wee bit more family friendly than Hunter. Still, the runs vary by experience with most diamond runs free of other skiers. Head here if you want a bit more solitude in your downhill.

getting there

If you're coming from Hunter Mountain take CR 6 to NY 42 N. From NY 42 N, take NY 23A E. Take a left at CR 17 (or, from the town of Hunter, take NY 23A until it intersects with CR 17). Turn right on NY 23 E. Turn right on CR 12. Take a right on Clarence D Lane Road. It's a 41-minute trip.

where to eat

Rock'n Mexicana. 5220 NY 23, Windham; (518) 734-3000. Situated at the Winwood Inn, Rock'n Mexicana offers interesting Mexican fare. Some of the items may be familiar to anyone who's eaten at a general Mexican restaurant, but some of the items are a bit more innovative such as the Caldo de Res (stewed beef with crushed tomatoes, corn, and cilantro) or the Pollo Rostizado (split roasted chicken with fresh salsa and *cotija* cheese). The ambience isn't anything special except for the views. $$.

Seasons Restaurant. 36 CR 12, Windham; (518) 734-3000. Situated 2 miles east of the resort, Seasons Restaurant serves the local community as well as seasonal visitors. Steaks get top billing as do some Italian dishes, all creating some interesting flourishes. Try the braised short ribs with butternut squash polenta or the roasted quail with corn bread and foie gras stuffing. The ambience is homey but a bit refined. $$$.

Waffle Cabin. If you're looking for food on the go, head to Waffle Cabin near the D-Lift. This small chain creates authentic Belgian waffles that are so buttery and rich, they slide off your tongue. The restaurant also serves hot apple cider. $.

where to stay

Winwood Inn and Condominiums. 5220 NY 23, Windham; (518) 734-3000. Situated just 1 mile from the resort, Winwood Inn and Condominiums offers well-appointed lodgings for couples, families, and groups. The standard suites have two double beds and private baths. The condos are a bit more luxurious with studio-style accommodations. Condos have kitchenettes, dining areas, and living rooms with sleeper sofas. Prices are reasonable, even in high season and during holiday weekends. $$$.

plattekill mountain

While Windham and Hunter get the most area skiers, Plattekill offers enough runs—some more challenging than others—to thrill skiers of all ages. Situated in Roxbury Road, Plattekill offers a smaller, more intimate ski experience than nearby resort areas and is decidedly more family centric. The 35 trails run the gamut from steep trails to a two-mile beginner's run (most of the trails are for mid-level skiers). The double diamond is a 1,100-foot vertical and is considered the steepest in the area. Snowboarders are welcome and for those who don't like to ski, there's always snow tubing. Kids under 7 ski for free.

getting there

From Windham, take CR 12 to NY 23 W. Turn left onto NY 30 S. Turn right at Cold Spring Road. Take a left at Upper Meeker Hollow Road. Turn left onto Lower Meeker Hollow Road. Take a left to New Kingston Mountain Road. The trip should take about 45 minutes.

where to eat

Cassie's Cafe. 53535 NY 30, Roxbury; (607) 326-7020. This local spot is known for its simple, yet hearty fare. Much of the food at Cassie's Cafe is made fresh daily on the premises, from the burgers (the meat is ground fresh) to the delicious turkey breast and roast beef. The atmosphere is welcoming if sometimes the staff can be a little curt to nonlocals. $.

East Branch Cafe. Main Street, NY 30, Roxbury; (607) 326-7763. This no-frills pizzeria serves a variety of standard pies as well as traditional Italian entrees. Try the pesto chicken pizza with bell peppers. The restaurant accommodates large parties such as families. Locals flock here in the summer for the outdoor seating with views of the East Branch of the Delaware River. $$.

where to stay

Stone Tavern Farm. 2080 Upper Meeker Hollow Rd., Roxbury; (607) 326-3600. Located 1 mile from the mountain, Stone Tavern Farm is a historic bed-and-breakfast that doubles as a horse farm and stables during the warmer weather. Built in 1803, the main house has 2 suites for guests. The first is for couples and features a woodburning fireplace and homey furnishings. The second suite is for large groups or families. The 3 bedrooms have a king bed, a queen, and 2 twins. Breakfast consists of eggs, bacon, and sausage. All the ingredients are fresh from the farm itself. Be sure to try the pancakes, which are a house specialty. The hotel requires a two-night minimum stay. $$$.

belleayre mountain

Since the early 1950s, Belleayre Mountain has been entertaining skiers of all levels and ages. The original site had 5 trails and New York's first chairlift. Today, the resort, operated by the New York State Department of Environmental Conservation, has 47 trails and 8 lifts, making it one of the largest ski resorts in the Catskills. There are quite a few beginner runs, but if you're an intermediate skier, you'll get the majority of the powder. There are also plenty of black diamond runs to challenge experts. The resort also has cross-country trails. Discounts apply throughout the season, but more often during late January and early February.

getting there

From Plattekill Mountain, take NY 30 S to CR 38. Take a right on CR 38 and a left to NY 28 S.

where to eat

Peekamoose Restaurant. 8373 NY 28, Big Indian; (845) 254-6500. Long heralded as the best restaurant in the Catskills, The Peekamoose Restaurant is just 2½ miles from Belleayre Mountain. Situated in a farmhouse overlooking a lovely creek, the rustic restaurant features exposed beams, hardwood floors, as well as a large dining room, tap room, and lounge. The innovative menu focuses on ingredients from local farmers and purveyors. The menu is always changing, but recent favorites included roast Muscovy duck with mission figs in a port demi-glace and free-range organic chicken sprinkled with cardamom. $$$.

Pine Hill Arms Restaurant. 225 Main St., Pine Hill; (845) 254-4012. A casual place at which to enjoy a good meal with good company. Pine Hill Arms has been touted by *Ski Magazine* as one of the best casual dining restaurants in the ski area. It's hard to dispute that claim when the restaurant is filled to capacity every night during ski season. The interior features wooden beams, low lighting, a large wooden bar at which to grab a drink or a gab, and a fireplace lounge. The food is solid with filling fare such as pecan-crusted sea bass and Mediterranean salmon as house specialties. $$$.

where to stay

Belleayre Lodge and Cabins. 15 Hostel Dr., Pine Hill; (845) 254-4200. Just a stone's throw from the mountain, Belleayre Lodge and Cabins offers efficiencies for large groups and families as well as smaller cabins for couples. The affordable one-room cottages are perfect for couples. These rustic cabins come equipped with kitchenettes and gas grills as well as TVs and Wi-Fi. The condo-esque cabin suite has two bedrooms, a wrap-around porch, and gas grill and fireplace. It's quite a bit more modern than the cottages. The main house has a game room as well as a fire pit at which you can meet other guests. $–$$.

south >>>

day trip 01

south

of brotherly love & history:
philadelphia, pennsylvania

What New York-based day-trip book would be complete without mentioning Philadelphia? Just 2 hours away, it offers as much culture and history as New York but at a much smaller scale. Still, there is so much to see and do in Philadelphia that it merits its own day trip even though you'll need more than a day to see all the sites.

Philly is one of the most walkable cities in the country, with a plethora of paths situated around historic sites. The city boasts a number of quaint, historic neighborhoods surrounding small parks—Rittenhouse Square, Washington Square, Fitler Square to name a few. Elfreth's Alley is the oldest continually-occupied street in the United States. The Old City District is the most historic mile in the country. Foundries and factories were transformed into residential buildings, galleries, bars, and clubs. It's quite reminiscent of the Williamsburg section of Brooklyn.

The wealth of museums is almost overwhelming. Most are of a historic nature and all are worth a detour. Most visitors start at Independence Mall, home to the Liberty Bell and Independence Hall. The city is fast becoming a culinary hotspot, due to the influx of celebrity chefs. Philly has long been known as a rock mecca, thanks to hundreds of music venues scattered throughout the city. These clubs are less pretentious than what you find in New York, and a night out here won't break the bank.

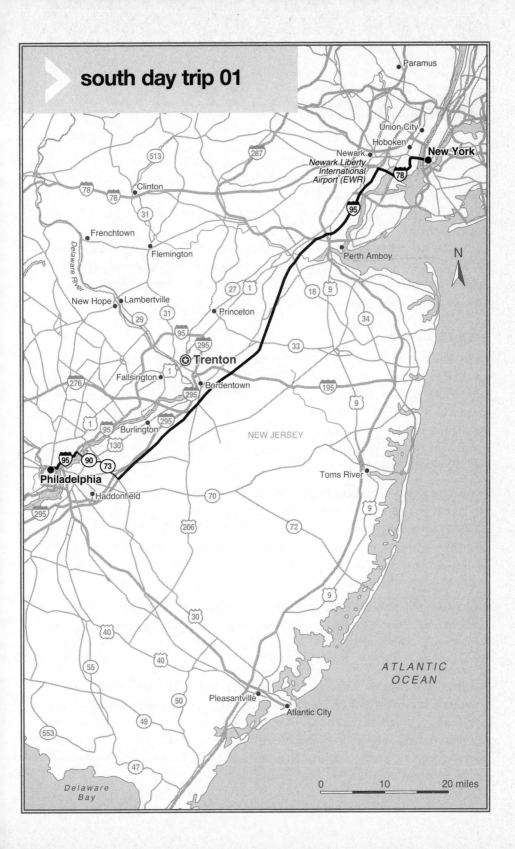

south day trip 01

philadelphia

getting there

Amtrak runs regular daily service from New York City's Penn Station to Philadelphia's 30th Street Station. The trip takes about 1 hour and 22 minutes on average. Once you get to 30th Street, hopping on the Southeastern Pennsylvania Transportation Authority (SEPTA) trains is a breeze.

By car, take the Holland Tunnel to I-78 S. Connect to I-95 S in Newark. Most of this is a toll road via the New Jersey Turnpike. Stay on the Turnpike until you reach US 73. Take US 73 west toward US 90 and connect to I-95 S again via the Betsy Ross Bridge. It will take approximately 2 hours.

where to go

Betsy Ross House. 239 Arch St., Philadelphia; (215) 686-1252. This 18th-century bandbox-style house was home to America's first flag maker. The city of Philadelphia acquired the home in 1941, and it's now run by the nonprofit Historic Philadelphia, Inc. Seven rooms with period furnishings and reproductions are on display including an upholstery shop much like the one used by Betsy Ross to make the flag. Tours are conducted throughout the day, and visitors are encouraged to relax in the courtyard and hear stories and see reenactments of colonial life.

Boathouse Row. 1 Boathouse Row, Philadelphia. Head here during the spring and summer to watch several annual regattas, the Independence Day Regatta being the largest. It's an amazing exercise in precision and stamina. Boathouse Row houses 15 different boathouses, some more than 150 years old, for various schools and rowing clubs. A public boathouse, Lloyd Hall, was built at the end of the row so that visitors can rent equipment to paddle on the river.

Edgar Allan Poe National Historical Site. 7 Spring Garden St., Philadelphia; (215) 597-8780. American literary legend Edgar Allan Poe's rented home doubles as a homage to his masterpieces. The museum features an art display, biographical film, mural, raven statue, and a collection of his poems. Admission is free.

Independence Hall. 520 Chestnut St., Philadelphia. This UNESCO World Heritage Site is the centerpiece of all American History. The Georgian building was erected in 1732 and completed 21 years later. It is here that both the Declaration of Independence and The Constitution were drafted. The tower is undergoing an extensive renovation so visits are prohibited. Free tours are conducted throughout the day but tickets need to be procured early in the day.

Liberty Bell Center. 600 Chestnut St., Philadelphia; (215) 965-2305. One of the most popular monuments in all of Philly, this 2,000-pound copper and tin bell was built in London in 1753. The original 44-pound clapper produced the famous crack and subsequent attempts to fix it failed. Housed in a new state-of-the-art center, visitors get a scientific look at the crack and how the bell works. Exhibits around the center show its historical significance.

National Constitution Center. 525 Arch St., Philadelphia; (215) 409-6600. This 160,000-square-foot interactive museum is entirely dedicated to the US Constitution. Exhibits include *Lincoln: The Constitution and the Civil War,* 42 statues of the men who signed and refused to sign the document, and an interactive film and live theater production about the signing.

National Museum of American Jewish History. 101 South Independence Mall East, Philadelphia; (215) 923-3811. Documenting the 350-year history of the Jewish Diaspora, this 100,000-square-foot museum features state-of-the-art interactive exhibits, paintings of Jewish life, and religious and cultural artifacts. Group tours are available.

Mutter Museum. 19 South 22nd St., Philadelphia; (215) 563-3737. Renowned for its creepy collection of human and animal anomalies, the Mutter Museum is not for the faint of heart but prides itself on educating the public about rare medical conditions. Specimens from famous peoples such as John Wilkes Booth are on view. The shrunken head and "Soap Lady" displays are particularly interesting. The latter is a petrified body that turned into soap.

Philadelphia Museum of Art. 2154 Benjamin Franklin Pkwy., Philadelphia; (215) 763-8100. This expansive museum, one of the nation's finest, has 200 galleries featuring permanent and temporary exhibits. From Renaissance works to Dada masterpieces, you'll find it all here. Of particular note are the Japanese tea house, medieval cloister, and pre-modern South Asian Temple hall. The museum hosts lectures and films throughout the year. Guided tours of the permanent collections as well as special exhibits are held throughout the day.

Please Touch: Museum for Children. 4231 Avenue of the Republic, Philadelphia; (215) 581-3181. If you've got a rowdy child, head to this children's museum that is sure to appease even the most temperamental tot. The 38,000-square-foot space houses six educational, interactive exhibits. Kids learn about water currents, transportation, and space in a fun, engaging way. Discount admission via Philadelphia CityPass.

Rodin Museum. 22nd Street and Benjamin Franklin Parkway, Philadelphia; (215) 568-6026. Opened in 1929, the Rodin Museum was the brainchild of Jules E. Maustbaum, a philanthropist and theater tycoon. The museum boasts 124 Auguste Rodin bronze, marble, and plaster masterpieces, including *The Thinker* and *The Burghers of Calais*. The museum's garden gets thousands of visitors a year. Visitors are encouraged to pay $5 for admission.

gardens of eden

*New York City has several notable botanical gardens, but **Longwood Gardens** (1001 Longwood Rd., Kennett Square, Pennsylvania; www.longwoodgardens .org) near Philadelphia is one of the most beautiful gardens in the world. Just 45 minutes south of the city, the gardens offer more than a thousand acres of plants, trees, and other horticultural delights. Visitors can roam through 20 indoor and 20 outdoor gardens year-round, thanks to the foresight of the Pierce family and Pierre du Pont. The Pierce family bought the existing farm and land from William Penn in 1700, and their descendents were the first to see the inherent beauty in the natural landscape, building an arboretum in 1798. Industrialist Pierre du Pont bought the property in 1906 and spent the next 30 years planting shrubs and cottage-garden flowers and building beautiful trellises and fountains, some landscaped, some more primeval. Much of the sweeping estate has a French and Italian influence. The Italian Water Garden, Topiary Garden and Analemmatic Sundial, and Oak and Conifer Knoll are particularly beautiful.*

where to shop

Kiki Hughes. 259 South 21st St., Philadelphia; (215) 546-1534. Located just west of Rittenhouse Square, this women's boutique has a unique selection of designer clothing, shoes, accessories and gifts. The hardwood floors and chandeliers give it a boudoir feel, and you'll love spending time going through the racks of clothes lining the walls. Clothing lines include Babette, Lilith and Cop Copine.

SA VA. 1700 Sansom St., Philadelphia; (215) 587-0004. Local fashionistas head to SA VA for its au courant designs and staples. Owner Sarah Van Aken creates many of the garments on sale at her on-site studio and other items are from organic or recycled sources. Prices are fairly reasonable. The jewelry by local fashion icon Bela Shehu is worth the visit alone.

Sioux Zanne Messix. 54½ North Third St., Philadelphia; (215) 928-9250. Situated in Old City amid landmarks, this chic and feminine boutique sells new and vintage baubles, women's clothing, and accessories. The jewelry is designed by owner Sioux Zanne. Zanne uses recycled items as well as hardware and semi-precious stones to create her one-of-a-kind pieces.

Topstitch Boutique. 54 North Third St., Philadelphia; (215) 238-8877. This young store in Old City features an artsy blend of clothing, jewelry, and handbags, all from local designers. Co-owner Linda Smyth creates hand-dyed leather earrings that she sells on the premises.

where to eat

Amada. 217 Chestnut St., Philadelphia; (215) 625-2450. Since 2005, Iron Chef Jose Garces has been delighting locals with his earthy, modern tapas. Garces reinterprets age-old recipes and judging by the lines out the door, he's doing something right. House specialties include lobster paella and suckling pig. The restaurant serves seasonal sangrias and offers a 40-bottle wine list, specializing in Spanish varietals. $$.

Barclay Prime. 237 South 18th St., Philadelphia; (215) 732-7560. Famous for its $100 cheesesteak, this nouveau-American steakhouse on Rittenhouse Square serves some of the finest cuts of beef around. Kobe sliders and butter-poached lobster are also house favorites. The clubby atmosphere makes for a warm and inviting experience. $$$.

City Tavern. 138 South Second St., Philadelphia; (215) 413-1443. This historic tavern served many of our founding fathers but went through tough times—a devastating fire in 1834, bad ownership—before it was taken over by chef/owner Walter Staib in 1994. Today, it's one of Philadelphia's dining stars, with an intimate feel and a menu of reinterpreted favorites. Guests can dine in one of the seven dining rooms or al fresco in the restaurant's garden. $$.

Lacroix at The Rittenhouse Hotel. 210 West Rittenhouse Sq., Philadelphia; (215) 790-2533. This elegant and refined eatery earns warranted accolades—"The World's Best Hotel Dining Room"—for its inventive international cuisine. Chef Jean-Marie Lacroix creates mouthwatering dishes, combining ingredients from around the world. The menu is fairly extensive, making it hard to choose a dish or two. Try the mussels and gnocchi gratin or the diver scallops with a chipotle date reduction. $$$.

Le Bec Fin. 1523 Walnut St., Philadelphia; (215) 567-1000. Francophiles will delight in this elegant French restaurant that has been a Philly mainstay for almost 40 years. If you have money to burn, splurge on the 9-course Grand Degustation menu. You can't go wrong with Hudson Valley foie gras or an escargots cassoullete. The fish and meat selections are varied and hearty. Try the poached rabbit loin or succulent Wagyu beef. Don't skip dessert, even if you don't have room. $$$.

Pod. 3636 Sansom St., Philadelphia; (215) 387-1803. Located in University City, this pan-Asian eatery caters to a young, hip crowd in search of a unique dining experience. Sit in private egg-shaped dining areas that change color or on stools that light up. A conveyor belt of dim sum and sushi slide past at the bar. $$.

The Ranstead Room. 2013 Ranstead St., Philadelphia. Head down Ranstead Street near Rittenhouse Square and look for the door marked with double "Rs." It's here you'll find restaurateur Stephen Starr's speakeasy-esque, The Ranstead Room. The Ranstead serves classic cocktails with a modern twist. Hand-cut ice, fresh squeezed juices, and homemade mixers make for a bespoke drinking experience. $$$.

where to stay

Alexander Inn. 301 South 12th St., Philadelphia; (215) 923-3535. A popular affordable hotel in Center City, the Alexander Inn welcomes single travelers, as well as couples and families. Single rooms are fairly barebones with a twin bed and sitting area. The doubles have more space and pretty views from bay windows. Service is attentive without being obsequious. The location is enough to sell the hotel. A free breakfast buffet is available every day. $.

Hotel Palomar Philadelphia. 117 South 17th St., Philadelphia; (215) 563-5006. A LEED Gold Certified hotel, the Hotel Palomar in Center City offers 230 rooms and suites, 19 of which are spa rooms. Rooms are modern and chic, in neutral tones with splashes of mauve and green, and are outfitted with zebra-print Frette linens, luxurious comforters, and bathrooms with recycled glass. The hotel is committed to sustainability. Furnishings were made with eco-friendly materials, rooms have on-site recycling bins and low-flow toilets. $$$.

Morris House Hotel. 225 South Eighth St., Philadelphia; (215) 922-2446. The Morris House hotel is one of Philly's most charming boutique properties. The brick colonial building is situated 2 blocks from Independence Hall in the Society Hill section of historic downtown Philly. The 15 rooms and suites offer bed-and-breakfast style ambience but with modern amenities. Beds are enveloped in 600-thread-count sheets and bathrooms are equipped

a step into the past

Colonial sites dot the landscape from Connecticut down to Southern Pennsylvania. **Valley Forge National Historic Park** *(PA 23 and North Gulph Road, Valley Forge, Pennsylvania; 610-783-1077; www.nps.gov/vafo) is significant and a can't-miss stop for any Revolutionary War Buff. It's here that General Washington transformed his constitutional army into a legendary force. Docents will tell you of the many soldiers who were African American and Native American and that 2,000 of the 5,000 troops met their death at the site, not through warfare, but due to a long, brutal winter. Visitors are treated to reenactments, kid-centric minicamps, and trolley and dinner tours.*

with Egyptian cotton linens. Continental breakfast is included in room rates. Make sure to head downstairs for daily afternoon tea service. $$.

The Rittenhouse. 210 West Rittenhouse Sq., Philadelphia; (215) 546-9000. One of the most prestigious hotels in the city, The Rittenhouse offers spacious accommodations in one of the most coveted and historic locations in town. The 98 rooms and site have mahogany furniture, plush linens, and marble bathrooms with oversized tubs. $$$.

worth more time

Reading Terminal is worth a side trip. A converted train station, it's now an anchor to the convention center and a Hard Rock hotel. Amish farmers bring their produce to sell at the indoor market. If you have a car take a jaunt to Longwood Gardens. This botanical wonderland is just 40 to 45 minutes south of the city. Historic Valley Forge is 45 minutes from Philly and can be biked to if you're adventurous. Just head through Manayunk along the canal towpath and pick up the paved bike path that turns through Conshohoken and other towns until you see the signposts saying you've arrived.

day trip 02

south

quaker roots:
bordentown, new jersey
burlington, new jersey

The Quakers were some of the first settlers in the United States and in many towns in South Jersey, Quaker roots run deep. John Farnsworth was the first European to make Bordentown, a quaint village on the banks of the Delaware River in Burlington County, home. The town, only a square-mile long, boasts about 40 historically significant homes and businesses as well as charming shops and restaurants. Ten miles away, Burlington has a rich Quaker history as well. The religious group established their first congregation in the town in 1678. It's here that William Penn ratified the Radical Constitution of West Jersey. Burlington is larger and more bustling than Bordentown. Even the most stalwart will find it hard to hit all the sites in one day.

bordentown

Patriot pride runs deep in this town of 4,000 residents. A number of Revolutionary War heroes lived here, including hometown hero Thomas Paine, and the village was an epicenter for patriot activities during the war. Unfortunately, the red coats burned it down in 1778. It was rebuilt soon after and saw an influx of European settlers, most notably Napoleon's brother Joseph Bonaparte and Clara Barton, founder of the American Red Cross. Today it teems with a local populace that is as friendly as it is helpful. Although many of the historic buildings are private homes and businesses and not available for a tour, they are still worth a detour.

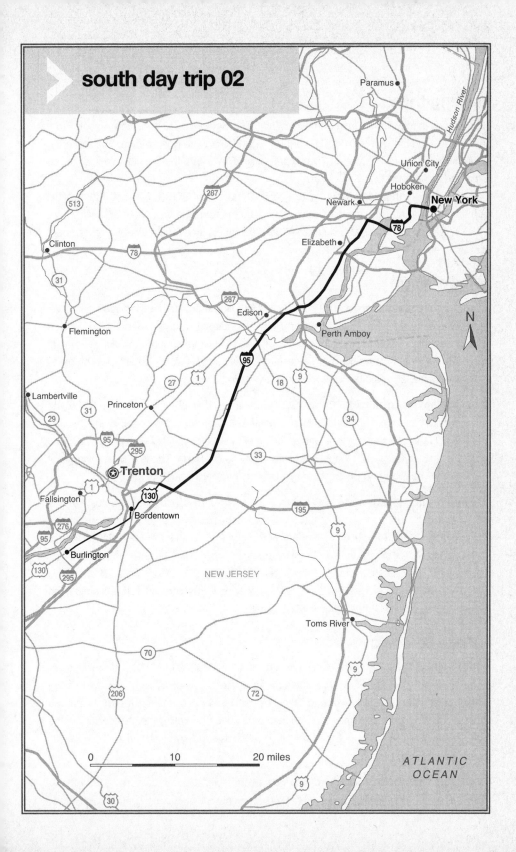

getting there

Take a New Jersey Transit train from New York Penn Station to Trenton, New Jersey. From Trenton take a New Jersey Transit River Line Light Rail train to Bordentown. The entire trip takes about an hour and a half (75 minutes for the NYC–Trenton leg, 11 minutes for the Trenton-Bordentown leg).

By car, take the Holland Tunnel to I-78 S. Connect to I-95 S in Newark. Most of this is a toll road via the New Jersey Turnpike. Stay on the Turnpike until you reach exit 7A for I-195 W. Connect to US 130 S via exit 5A. Take a right on Crosswicks Street. It takes about the same amount of time as the train.

where to go

Clara Barton Schoolhouse. 142 Crosswicks St., Bordentown. This brick colonial building is where the founder of the American Red Cross taught neighborhood children whose parents' couldn't afford to pay school tuition. It was the first free public school in the United States. It features a desk and chair, a cast iron stove, and a low bench at which students sat. A second floor exists but isn't available for viewing.

Joseph Hopkinson House. 63 Park St., Bordentown. Joseph Hopkinson, author of the anthem "Hail Columbia" and a U.S. Representative, once called this house home (he was the son of Francis Hopkinson, one of the signers of the Declaration of Independence). It also served as the residence of Joseph Bonaparte's private physician. This is a great example of Flemish style as laid bond bricks were used on the original sections of the building.

Thomas Paine House. White Hart Street, Bordentown. English Quaker Thomas Paine is considered by many to be one of the most important figures in American history and as much a father of the Revolution as George Washington. His books *Common Sense, Age of Reason,* and *Rights of Man* were bestsellers during his lifetime and are still considered political classics today (although *Age of Reason* ruined his reputation). Paine called Bordentown home and the town has a statue erected in his honor on Prince Street. His home on Church Street is now a dentists' office but is worth a visit.

where to shop

Artful Deposit, Inc. 201 Farnsworth Ave., Bordentown; (609) 298-6970. This small gallery showcases a wide array of local artists including the late Joseph William Dawley, Expressionist artist Hanneke de Neve, and Gennady Spirin. Much of the work depicts bucolic scenes and landscapes. Owner C.J. Mugavero has been operating the gallery since 1986 and has accumulated an impressive collection of diverse and talented works. The gallery is open Wed through Sun.

Old Book Shop of Bordentown. 200 Farnsworth Ave., Bordentown; (609) 324-9909. This antiquarian bookstore houses 10,000 first-edition, rare, and out-of-print books. Much of the selection focuses on American history and culture as well as the military and New Jersey history. A first edition of *The Adventures of Huckleberry Finn* goes for $3,250. A small children's selection delights kids of all ages.

Record Collector. 358 Farnsworth Ave., Bordentown; (609) 324-0880. Vinyl junkies will spontaneously combust in this small but well-stocked store. For more than 25 years, Record Collector has been stocking its shelves with a vast array of new and used LPs, 7-inches, 45s, and CDs and has been earning accolades around the world for that collection. With more than a million titles to choose from, you could spend an entire day at this store and still not be finished looking. The staff is friendly and knowledgeable about all genres of music. The store also boasts a music venue that showcases world-renowned acts on weekends.

where to eat

Farnsworth House. 135 Farnsworth Ave., Bordentown; (609) 291-9232. A homey and hearty spot on the main drag. This fine dining Mediterranean restaurant, housed in a Revolutionary War–era building, earns raves for its well-made Italian staples and huge portions. Order the Speedino ala Farnsworth. The prosciutto and mozzarella dish is delectable as is the Coquelle St. Jacques. The beer list is long and well thought out. $$.

HOB Tavern. 146 Second St., Bordentown; (609) 291-7020. If you want an inexpensive but homey meal, head to this historic restaurant away from the more touristy stretch of town. HOB aka Heart of Bordentown Tavern serves pub favorites, from sweet potato fries to roast beef sandwiches to simple dishes named for famous locals such as Clara Barton, Thomas Paine, and William Allen. Karaoke Saturdays are always packed. $$.

Oliver a Bistro. 218 Farnsworth Ave., Bordentown; (609) 298-7177. A local BYOB favorite, Oliver a Bistro serves an eclectic array of dishes, many Latin-, Asian-, or Mediterranean-inspired, in an elegant atmosphere. The appetizers are local favorites, including the truffle mushroom bruschetta, and pear and pecan salad with port wine vinaigrette. The 4-course tasting menu (available Tues through Fri nights) is a steal, especially considering the generous portions. $$.

Under the Moon. 316 Farnsworth Ave., Bordentown; (609) 291-8301. This diner-cum-store serves heaping portions of modern American favorites with some Latin flavors thrown in for good measure. The atmosphere is decidedly fun, with antiques, tchotchkes, and homey accents. The service is attentive and very friendly. Menu highlights included the Oaxaca guacamole and beef Wellington. Desserts are decadent and shouldn't be missed. The restaurant is BYOB. $$.

where to stay

Inn at Fernbrook Farms. 142 Bordentown-Georgetown Rd., Bordentown; (609) 298-3868. This beautiful, 7-bedroom inn dates back to the mid-1700s but has been owned by the Kuser family since 1890. The house has 30 rooms for guests to relax in, whether it's to enjoy a book or a coze or play billiards. Stroll through the gardens and farmland. Rooms have restored antiques, wrought iron headboards, and homemade quilts and shams. Pets are welcome with advance notice. $$.

burlington

Besides being known for James Lawrence, the town was also home to Ulysses S. Grant and *The Last of the Mohicans* author James Fenimore Cooper. Burlington was an important industrial mecca for many years and a stop on the Underground Railroad. Six of the town's historic buildings and structures played a role in helping slaves escape the south.

getting there

Thanks to New Jersey Transit's River Line, it's a quick 13-minute ride on the light rail from Bordentown Station to Burlington Towne Center Station. By car from Bordentown, take Farnsworth Avenue to US 130 S. Take a right on Columbus Road. It's a 15-minute drive.

where to go

Burlington Island. Site of the first settlement in the state (ca. 1624), Burlington Island has Belgian, Dutch, Swedish, Finnish, and English roots. Throughout its nearly 400-year-history, it's played host to recreational activities including an amusement park, beach, and bathhouse. Only accessible by boat, the 300-acre island is now an education site monitored by the Board of Island Managers. The amusement park was dredged and a lagoon was created. It has miles of good hiking trails, and the overseers will finally allow visitors to kayak on the lake.

Grubb Estate. 46 Riverbank, Burlington. Currently privately owned, the Grubb Estate has special historical significance. Owner Henry Grubb allegedly built tunnels under his home to help runaway slaves flee the south during The Civil War. The estate has two Victorian-style homes on-site and once boasted a tannery as well as a brewery.

James Fenimore Cooper House. 457 High St., Burlington. Built in 1780, the house is the birthplace of *The Last of the Mohicans* novelist James Fenimore Cooper and is now home to the Burlington Historical Society. The home contains 4 rooms of documents, pictures, and artifacts. Some of the items in the collection belonged to Joseph Bonaparte.

Ulysses S. Grant House. 309 Wood St., Burlington. Former president and Civil War general Ulysses S. Grant transported his family to Burlington during the war in 1864 to avoid the pain and pressure of the conflict. They lived in the home for only a year. It is now a private residence but worth a peek from the outside.

where to shop

Historic Burlington Antiques and Art Emporium. 424 High St., Burlington; (609) 747-8333. This 14,000-square-foot gallery hosts a steady stream of visitors due to its extensive collection of vintage art, antiques, and collectibles from 65 area dealers. One could spend two days just strolling through the myriad stalls. Many of the items are affordable and most dealers will hold items and transport them within a 50-mile radius for a small fee. Coffee and tea are served free daily.

Philips Furniture and Antiques. 307 High St., Burlington; (609) 386-7125. Considered one of the best shops in town, this 3-story emporium has a wide array of vintage and rare collectibles. Customers can choose from sofas, chairs, bedroom furniture, and a unique number of wardrobe units. The shop also sells ceramics, books, and rare glass.

where to eat

Amy's Omelette House Burlington Diner. 637 High St., Burlington; (609) 386-4800. If you've gone to Cafe Gallery for brunch and miss your eggs, head to this expansive diner, which specializes in omelettes (there are 137 varieties on the menu) and other egg dishes. The selection is beyond extensive. Try the French brie omelette. The combination of fruit, nuts, honey, and brie makes it both savory and satisfying. Carousel horses and model sailboats make the diner feel a bit more fun. $$.

Blue Claw Crab Eatery. 1101 US 130, Burlington; (609) 387-3700. Since 1961, this casual seafood restaurant has been drawing the crowds. The affordable menu is fairly standard with broiled and fried fish as well as chicken, ribs, mussels, and clams. The restaurant is known for its extensive menu of crab dishes, from blue to snow to dungeness to king. Kids are taken care of and encouraged to draw on tables. $$.

Cafe Gallery. 219 High St., Burlington; (609) 386-6150. Enjoy a view of the Delaware River at this continental restaurant housed in a Federalist building. The romantic eatery features an ever-changing display of fine art. Sunday brunch is particularly fantastic and features a number of unique dishes (don't expect eggs and bacon). Prices are a little steep for the quality but you're paying for the view, so what can you expect? $$.

where to stay

The Lilly Inn. 214 High St., Burlington; (609) 526-7900. A 300-year-old brick colonial building in the heart of town, just 2 blocks from the River Line train station. Guests have a choice of 5 bedrooms, all with high ceilings, hardwood floors, blue marble fireplaces, and restored antiques. The Mary Smith room, which overlooks the garden, is the most romantic choice. The inn welcomes pets, for an additional fee and offers AARP and military discounts. Guests who stay for more than two days get additional discounts. $$.

day trip 03

south

>>> **on the waterfront:**
haddonfield, new jersey
collingswood, new jersey

In recent years, southern Jersey has seen a renaissance of sorts and two towns are at the forefront of that resurgence. Haddonfield's downtown is one of the most thriving in the Philadelphia environs. Most shops are independently owned and many of the area restaurants are BYO (due to strict liquor laws). The colonial-style architecture and tree-lined streets appease history buffs. Collingswood is in the same vein. All restaurants are BYO, and the town's historic quarter hosts dozens of street fairs, festivals, and events throughout the year making it an ideal romantic getaway. Their proximity to the Cooper River allows for scenic strolls and aquatic diversions.

haddonfield

Whether it's the first dinosaur skeleton found in the United States, romantic eateries, or cute mom-and-pop shops, Haddonfield offers something out of the ordinary. Originally settled in 1695, the town is steeped in tradition. Kings Highway, once a wagon trail for the British army, runs through the center of town bisecting the narrow tree-lined streets and their antique street lights. The walkable 4-block downtown district has more than 200 shops, galleries, and restaurants. But beware: the town, like 36 others in the state, has been 100 percent dry since 1873.

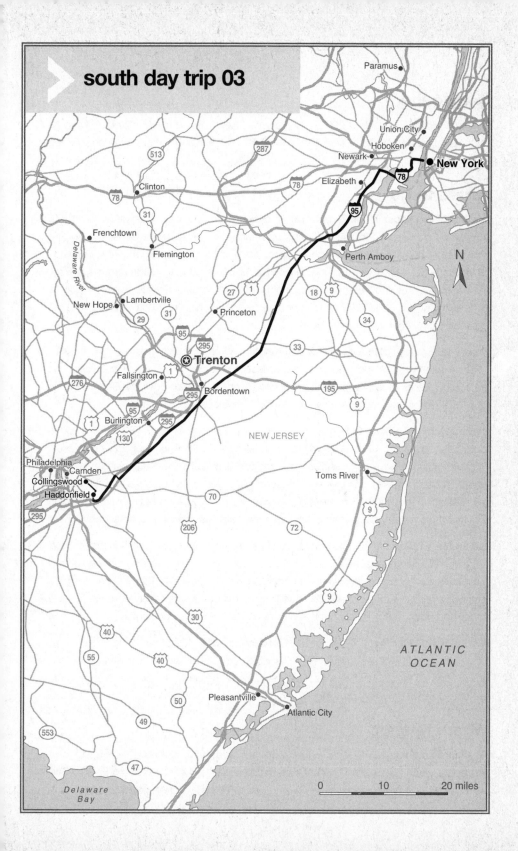

south day trip 03

getting there

Take the Holland Tunnel to I-95 S. Continue to New Jersey Turnpike South. After 43 miles, take exit 4 to NJ 73 N. Merge onto I-295 S. Take exit 30 for Warwick Road towards Haddonfield.

where to go

Haddonfield Dinosaur Commemorative Site. Maple Avenue, Haddonfield. In 1858, archaeologists digging through a clay pit on a farm discovered the remains of a 30-foot dinosaur, the first of its kind on North American soil. Dubbed *Hadrosaurus Foulkii,* or Haddy for short, the 73-million-year-old find heralded a rabid interest in fossilized remains. Today, the bones are on display at the Academy of Natural Sciences in Philadelphia but dinosaur buffs can visit the National Historic Landmark to view a plaque, stone markers, and an overlook commemorating the discovery.

Historical Society of Haddonfield. 343 Kings Hwy. East, Haddonfield; (856) 429-7375. At Greenfield Hall, this home possesses a collection of Victorian furniture, local glass, and colonial costumes as well as a collection of pottery and toys. Next door, the Samuel Mickle House stores the society's collection of historic homes and town records.

In the Kitchen Cooking School. 10 Mechanic St., Haddonfield; (845) 489-1682. If you're looking for something fun to do, head to this cooking school for gourmet cooking classes. Students learn to cook with and without recipes and plate them like world-renowned chefs. Cooking classes change regularly; one night you could prepare a hearty winter meal, another night it's French fare. Couples classes are offered regularly. All students dine together at the end of class. A small kitchen supply store is attached to the school.

Indian King Tavern. 233 Kings Hwy. East, Haddonfield; (856) 429-6792. This former hotel and public house saw the ratification of the Declaration of Independence by the New Jersey General Assembly and is also where the state's seal was adopted. Today it's no longer a watering hole but a museum. Guided free tours take visitors to a variety of rooms on two floors. The cellar, which is said to have private passageways, is inaccessible.

Markeim Arts Center. 104 Walnut St., Haddonfield; (856) 429-8585. Haddonfield's premier art gallery showcases a smattering of artwork and doubles as a school with workshops and art classes for artists of all ages. Opened in 1956, the center supports arts and culture in South Jersey, especially anything involving children and emerging artists.

where to shop

English Gardener. 125 Kings Hwy. East, Haddonfield; (856) 354-5051. Any East Coast Anglophile worth his weight in pence buys British goods and sundries at the English Gardener. From canned mushy peas to Guinness apparel to Rowntrees candies to P.G. Tips teas, the store stocks more than 3,000 items from across the pond and appeals to anyone looking for classic English goods and gifts. The store also offers free shipping on all orders in the United States.

The Owl's Tale. 140 Kings Hwy. East, Haddonfield; (856) 795-8110. Specializing in estate furniture and heirlooms, The Owl's Tale is the go-to antiques store in Haddonfield. The selection is top-notch and the prices and service can't be beat.

Secrets. 221A Kings Hwy. East, Haddonfield; (856) 354-9111. Consignment shops in New York City often have a hit or miss selection. Secrets is more hit than miss. You can find a variety of designer clothing, handbags, shoes, and other accessories at relatively affordable prices. The designer shoe selection alone is worth a visit.

where to eat

The Apron. 47 Kings Hwy. East, Haddonfield; (856) 795-4333. Comfort food gets top billing at this homey joint run by two friends. They use old family recipes and reinterpret them for today's healthier lifestyle. The chili and barbecue draws lines out the door, and the chicken pot pie is a personal favorite for its flaky crust and heaps of succulent chicken. The restaurant also hosts cooking classes for children and adults. $$.

British Chip Shop. 146 Kings Hwy. East, Haddonfield; (856) 354-0204. Decorated with photos from the British Isles and U.K. soccer replicas, this new addition to the Haddonfield food scene serves huge portions of made-to-order fried haddock and chips as well as more unique takes on the traditional takeaway (fried lump crab with lime mayo dipping sauce anyone?). Head here if you like mushy peas, P.G. Tips teas, scones, or bangers and mash but expect a bit of a wait. $$.

Veronica's Restaurant. 26 South Haddon Ave., Haddonfield; (856) 616-1520. Located off the main drag, Veronica's Restaurant still manages to do a brisk business largely due to its original take on Mediterranean cuisine. This isn't your typical Italian or Greek restaurant. Veronica's serves food typically found in the Balkans. While some menu items may seem familiar (falafel, baba ghanoush), some are dishes you could be trying for the first time (cevapi, mititei). $$.

where to stay

Haddonfield Inn. 44 West End Ave., Haddonfield; (856) 428-2195. A beautiful 9-room Victorian inn that caters to an older refined crowd. Rooms are elegantly appointed and focus on a particular destination. There's the Mediterranean blues and yellows of the Monaco Suite, the beachside sophistication of The Cape May Room, the wild and animal Safari room. All accommodations have comfortable beds, hypoallergenic comforters and pillows, fireplaces, and en suite bathrooms. $$.

collingswood

Haddonfield's neighbor to the west, Collingswood, has been called one of kindest places in New Jersey, and after spending a day enjoying the sights and sounds of town, you'll definitely concur. An eclectic downtown and a thriving BYO scene make for an affordable day visiting fine arts and crafts stores, high-end consignment shops, antiques galleries, and the 20 dining establishments—many of them ethnic—on Haddon Avenue, aka Restaurant Row. It's also noteworthy for its green spaces and walkability and bikability, so park the car and enjoy a day breathing in the fresh air as you watch the sailboats go by on the Cooper River.

getting there

From Haddonfield, take CR 561 north 2.5 miles to Collingswood. It's about a 5-minute drive, without traffic.

where to go

Collingswood Community Theatre. 315 White Horse Pike, Collingswood. Since 2002, the Collingswood Community Theatre has been staging four to five productions a year for the local community, featuring the local community (all actors must be Collingswood residents). The theater showcases musicals, dramas, and comedies at three sites around town: the Community Center, the Grand Ballroom, and the Scottish Rite Theatre.

Perkins Center for the Arts. 30 Irvin Ave., Collingswood; (856) 833-0009. A satellite facility for the larger 30-year old Perkins Center for the Arts in Moorestown, the Collingswood center opened in 2002. The green building has been restored to include exhibition spaces, art studios, and classrooms to enrich the lives and culture of the Collingswood community.

Scottish Rite Theater. 315 White Horse Pike, Collingswood; (856) 858-1000. This 75-year-old theater has played host to Broadway productions and concerts featuring legendary acts such as David Crosby, Ben Folds, and Joan Baez. Each concert seats more than a 1,000 people from around the area.

where to shop

Charm. 697 Haddon Ave., Collingswood; (856) 833-1697. Specializing in dresses, Charm is a quaint boutique that offers clothing, handbags, and accessories for women of all ages. Owner Dawn Burke Sena and her daughters comb through the latest fashion magazines to find trendy and stylish items. The shop also offers charm classes for teens.

Collingswood Farmers' Market. Between Collings and Irvin Avenues. Held every Saturday from May to Thanksgiving, the Collingswood Farmers' Market brings fresh produce directly from the farm to the citizens of this region. The market has become a Saturday morning tradition for the entire region. You'll find an abundance of seasonal produce grown and harvested by local South Jersey farmers as well as meats and baked goods.

Elizabeth Originals. 809 Haddon Ave., Collingswood; (856) 831-6518. This gallery and boutique boasts a wonderful collection of fine art, ceramics, handbags, scarves, jewelry, and other items. Owner Elizabeth Toplin-McShane prides herself on her collection of one-of-a-kind items. The framed oil pastel paintings are truly unique as they were created by Toplin-McShane herself.

Frugal Resale. 740 Haddon Ave., Collingswood; (856) 858-0700. One of the newest additions to the avenue, Frugal Resale is a family friendly consignment shop that specializes in affordable clothing and accessories. Children can play in a kids-only play area, and owner Morgan Robinson sponsors childbirth and parenting classes on-site.

Philly Stamp and Coin. 683 Haddon Ave., Collingswood; (856) 854-5333. This small, one-stop-shop buys, sells, appraises, and displays coins and stamps. The store also carries other accoutrements.

where to eat

Blackbird. 619 Collings Ave., Collingswood; (856) 854-3444. Known for its homemade pasta, this Franco-Italian restaurant is new to the Collingswood BYO scene. Chef Alex Capasso serves modern Mediterranean cuisine with an Asian influence. The chic 70-seat eatery has earned accolades for its gnocchi. $$.

Green House. 655 Haddon Ave., Collingswood; (856) 854-0896. Vegetarians will delight in this small, Asian eatery that creates creative meat-free fare at affordable prices. Choose from a wide array of appetizers and entrees, some with tofu. $$.

Joe Pesce. 833 Haddon Ave., Collingswood; (856) 833-9888. No, it's not named for the actor. *Pesce* is the Italian word for fish, and this restaurant specializes in fresh seafood from around the globe. The whole grilled fish is probably the best dish on the menu: flavorful and filling. The restaurant also serves meat, pasta, and poultry. $$.

Kitchen Consigliere Cafe. 8 Powell Ave., Collingswood; (856) 854-2196. Don't let the name scare you off. You won't run into Robert Duvall here. Authentic Italian cuisine gets top billing at this casual eatery off the main drag. Chef Angelo Lutz uses time-honored recipes, many from his mother and grandmother, to create hearty, filling dishes. $$.

day trip 04

south

>>> **a gambler's paradise:**
atlantic city, new jersey

Gambling is one of America's favorite pastimes (two thirds of the American population has gambled at some point). While many New York–area gamblers don't have the time or money to head to Monaco or Las Vegas, Atlantic City offers a fun alternative that is an easy jaunt no matter the time of year.

If you've played Monopoly, you're already familiar with the layout of Atlantic City. Located a little more than 2 hours away, Atlantic City is a resort community that has seen its share of ups and downs. The first seaside hotel was built in town in 1853, followed by the first boardwalk in 1870. Both were built to accommodate the throngs of tourists heading into Atlantic City—more than 500,000 a year by the late 1800s. Hotels sprouted up, and the town became a wealthy enclave.

If you've ever watched the HBO series, *Boardwalk Empire,* you've seen a fairly accurate depiction of Atlantic City during its heyday in the 1920s and '30s. During Prohibition, the city was a mecca of corruption, decadence, bootlegging, and general sinfulness. After World War II, the city went through a 60-year decline as many residents and developers left for greener pastures. Throughout the latter part of the century, Atlantic City saw an upsurge in crime and low high school graduation rates, and had a reputation as one of the most unsavory cities in the United States. While it's still unsafe in parts and suffers from high unemployment, it's worth a day trip if you want to enjoy tax-free shopping, good food, and gambling. Many of the casinos have a vintage feel to them, especially those near the Boardwalk, but several new hotel-casinos have been built further off the main drag to attract Las Vegas–style clientele. Has the city's fortunes changed? The jury is still out.

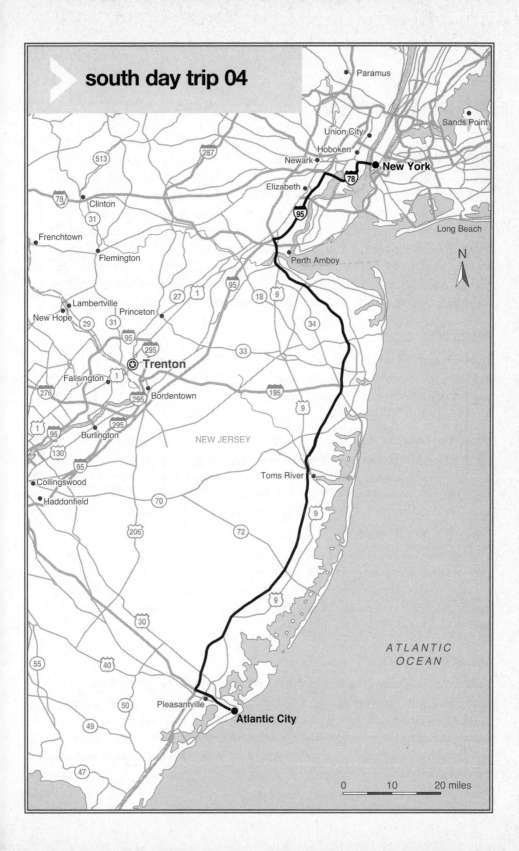

south day trip 04

atlantic city

getting there

Buses run regularly from Port Authority to specific casinos near the Boardwalk, and riders get a return on their tickets in either cash or casino vouchers once they arrive at their destination. You can also take the Aces Train to and from Atlantic City via Penn Station.

The best way to get here is by car as getting here is fairly straightforward and parking is cheap. The drive isn't as picturesque as other journeys into this part of New Jersey. You're trying to get to Atlantic City as quickly as possible. Take I-95 S via the Holland Tunnel. After 20 miles, take exit 11 to the Garden State Parkway S. Look for exit 38, which leads you onto the Atlantic City Expressway E. Look for signs for specific casino exits.

where to go

Abescon Lighthouse. Pacific and Rhode Island Avenues; (609) 449-1360. This 19th-century lighthouse stands more than 170 feet above the city skyline. Pretty impressive when you compare it to the massive casinos nearby. Visitors can admire the Atlantic City skyline as well as parts of the Jersey shore. Open June through Sept.

Boardwalk Hall. 2301 Boardwalk; (609) 348-7000. Once one of the largest buildings in the world, Boardwalk Hall has an impressive 82-year history. The Romanesque building served as an army training facility during World War II and has played host to numerous concerts and events including the annual Miss America pageant. The building went through an extensive renovation from 1998 to 2001 that created a new seating bowl, floor, and ice rink.

Lucy the Elephant. 9200 Atlantic Ave., Margate, New Jersey; (609) 823-6473. James Lafferty built this massive, 6-story, 90-ton Asian elephant in the 19th century. Over the years, the monument has served as an office and tavern. It was due to be demolished in the 1970s but locals fought to preserve the structure, which is now a National Historic Landmark and located down Atlantic Avenue in Margate, New Jersey. Guests are allowed to venture inside the monument and admire the ocean views.

where to shop

Atlantic City Outlets—The Walk. 1931 Atlantic Ave.; (609) 872-7002. Located at the end of the Atlantic City Expressway, the Atlantic City Outlets are one of the most popular shopping spots in the entire town. Here you'll find 100 high-end and low-end outlets for popular brands and stores including Adidas, American Eagle Outfitters, BCBG, Calvin Klein, and Old Navy. The complex also includes restaurants and features special events and sales throughout the year.

The Pier Shops at Caesars. One Atlantic Ocean; (609) 345-3100. The newest addition to the outlet-shopping scene, The Pier Shops at Caesars offers 80 Vegas-style emporiums and restaurants such as Bottega Veneta, Gucci, Hugo Boss, and Tiffany & Co. While the selection doesn't compare to the New York City outposts of said brands, you can still find deals, especially during seasonal sales.

The Quarter at Tropicana. 2831 Boardwalk; (609) 340-4000. Although smaller than The Walk and The Pier Shops, The Quarter still draws crowds because of the name brand shops and kitschy emporiums. Located on the main floor of the Tropicana casino, The Quarter houses 30 different shops. There's men's clothing mecca Brooks Brothers as well as pet emporium Jake's Dog House. The shops are a bit more unique than what you'll find elsewhere.

where to eat

Many of the best restaurants are located in casino-hotels. **The Borgata Casino Hotel & Spa** (1 Borgata Way) has several fine dining options. The best of the bunch includes **Izakaya** (609-317-1000; $$$), a Japanese restaurant known for its innovative takes on sushi. Try the edamame dumplings, miso-glazed eggplant, and giant clam sashimi. The decor is a mix of east and west with dramatic floral murals and shoji screens flanking tables. **Bobby Flay Steak** (609-317-1000; $$$) boasts classic steaks with Flay's signature Southwestern flair. Pesto is common condiment on both the appetizer and main course menu, which has the requisite steaks as well as seafood options. The ambience is ultra modern yet inviting.

Angelo's Fairmont Tavern. 2300 Fairmont Ave.; (609) 344-2439. Another historic eatery popular with locals and in-the-know tourists. The interior conjures up images of Italian villages. Part of the narrow space looks as if it's been transported from a quaint Italian alley. Angelo's has been voted the best Italian restaurant in town, and after having the chicken cacciatore, one can see why. $$.

Dock's Oyster House. 2405 Atlantic Ave.; (609) 345-0092. No day-tripper in Atlantic City should skip eating in the heart of town, away from the casinos. You'll meet locals and get a better lay of the land. Since 1897, tourists and locals have made Dock's Oyster House an institution. The seafood and steak restaurant is located just steps from the main drag. Guests dine on a wealth of fresh fish and shellfish. The raw bar menu is fairly priced. Try the shrimp ceviche or the wasabi tuna. The Doc's Classic menu features items that have been served at the eatery since its inception. The award-winning wine list features new and old world selections at reasonable prices. $$.

The Melting Pot. 2112 Atlantic Ave.; (609) 441-1100. One of Atlantic City's newest and most fun eateries (located just down the street from Dock's Oyster House), The Melting Pot serves a variety of fondues as well as salads and entrees. The spinach and artichoke fondue is a fan favorite. The restaurant hosts 4-course, fondue-centric evenings throughout the year. Gluten-free diners will thank the restaurant for offering wheat- and spelt-free dipping items. $$.

where to stay

Borgata Casino Hotel & Spa. 1 Borgata Way; (609) 317-1000. Since it opened in 2003, the Borgata Casino Hotel & Spa has earned raves and drawn tourists. Why? Because it's the best hotel in town. The Vegas-style ambience sets the tone. The lobby is large and welcoming, with VIPs treated as VIPs. The 2,000 carpeted rooms and suites are spacious and set in modern lines and neutral tones. Bathrooms have granite countertops and glass-enclosed showers. The hotel has a spa, indoor pool, and fitness center as well as 13 restaurants. But let's be real here. You come for the casino. The 161,000-square-foot casino floor is the largest in town. Guests can choose from a variety of table games such as blackjack, Texas Hold'em, and Pai Gow. There are also more than 4,000 slot machines. $$$$.

The Chelsea. 111 South Chelsea Ave.; (800) 548-3030. Not every hotel in Atlantic City has a casino attached or caters to a hedonistic crowd. The Chelsea is a Manhattan-style boutique hotel with a retro feel and no casino. Located on the water, the 20-story property caters to well-heeled customers as well as young couples looking for a hip and fun getaway. Rooms are separated into two categories: Chelsea Luxe and The Annex. The first are suites, all with sweeping views of the city or sea and bespoke linens and clean white lines. The latter are vintage-inspired, with retro tiles and views of the saltwater pool. The Chelsea also offers private beach access and cabana service as well as a rooftop bar, spa, and two restaurants. $$$.

day trip 05

south

>>>

the real jersey shore:
the wildwoods, new jersey
cape may, new jersey

Forget what you may have seen or heard about the Jersey shore. While the MTV show may make one think that the New Jersey seaside is full of overly-muscled and tanned idiots, much of the Jersey shoreline is replete with lovely towns at which to enjoy a summer day without running into undesirables. Two of the most fun are Cape May and The Wildwoods. The first has famous beaches, Victorian homes, and a wealth of cultural offerings. The latter is a confluence of family-friendly towns with top-rated beaches, unique retro architecture, and more than 180 free festivals throughout the year. While both see an influx of tourists in the summer, they are never as obnoxious as what you'd find in shore towns closer to New York City. (Cough*SeasideHeights*Cough.)

the wildwoods

While much of the Jersey shore is filled with drunken, college-aged kids during the summer, there are spots at which sun worshippers can unwind with family and not worry about "juiceheads" or their followers. The Wildwoods, a group of five seaside towns on the Island of Five Mile Beach on the base of the New Jersey shore, is one such family friendly destination. Much of the 5-mile beach offers amusements for kids of all ages. It's a bit like Coney Island but with a cleaner, more upscale feel. Rollercoasters, water slides, and monster truck races line the sand offering a host of activities that will keep even the most morose child entertained. But the Wildwoods are more than just a beach destination. The entertaining

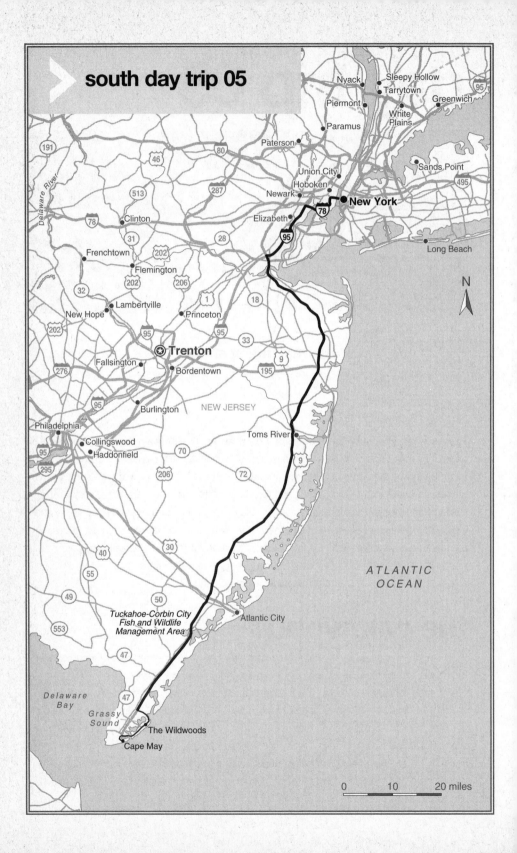

191

Nyack
Sleepy Hollow
Tarrytown
Piermont
Greenwich
Paramus
White
Plains
95
80
46
Paterson
Sands Point
513
287
495
Union City
Hoboken
Newark
New York
Clinton
78
Elizabeth
78
31
28
95
Frenchtown
202
Flemington
Long Beach
32
202
206
1
18
Lambertville
New Hope
Princeton
95
202
95
33
Trenton
9
Fallsington
195
Bordentown
276
9
95
Burlington
NEW JERSEY
Philadelphia
Collingswood
Haddonfield
70
Toms River
95
9
295
72
206
N

Delaware River

40
30
55
49
50
ATLANTIC
OCEAN
553
Tuckahoe-Corbin City
Fish and Wildlife
Management Area
Atlantic City
47

Delaware
Bay
47
Grassy
Sound
The Wildwoods
Cape May

0   10   20 miles

towns feature unique Doo Wop architecture as well as a variety of good dining options that make a day trip worth the drive.

getting there

Take the Holland Tunnel to I-95 S. Take exit 11 to the Garden State Parkway S. Take exit 6 to Whiteboro/North Wildwood. Turn right onto North Wildwood Boulevard/NJ 147. It's about a 2½ hour drive.

where to go

The Wildwoods Boardwalk. Playfully dubbed "two miles of smiles," the Wildwoods Boardwalk is part of a dying breed. Fewer and fewer pristine seaside boardwalks exist in the United States. For more than 100 years, it has played host to millions of visitors, who've walked its length to admire the many kitschy shops and amusements such as rollercoasters, water parks, and tramcars. It flanks one of the loveliest 5-mile beaches in New Jersey. The beach is free to locals and tourists, and visitors often enjoy sailing, whale watching, kayaking, and laying on the white sand.

Boardwalk Sightseer Tram Cars. Originally built for the 1939 World's Fair in New York City, the Sightseer Tram Cars are electric-powered, eco-friendly vehicles that shuttle visitors from one end of the boardwalk to the other. Millions of people have ridden the cars in the more than 60 years of operation, with 500,000 visitors annually.

Doo Wop Experience Museum and Neon Sign Garden. Ocean Avenue between Burk and Montgomery Avenues. If you want to learn more about mid-century architecture and culture, the Doo Wop Experience and Neon Sign Garden is worth a visit. The museum celebrates the era's architecture, music, and popular culture. The Wildwoods area was a popular destination during the 1950s and '60s, and thankfully, many of the buildings from that time still stand in the historic district. A garden takes restored neon signs and displays them in an amazing array. The museum also hosts a Doo Wop Bus tour on Tuesday and Thursday nights during the summer. The educational tour takes visitors through the historic district to admire the mid-century industrial architecture. The museum also houses a vintage-inspired malt shop and gift shop.

Hereford Inlet Lighthouse. 111 North Central Ave., North Wildwood; (609) 522-4520. Like other lighthouses in the area, the Hereford Inlet Lighthouse has been assisting mariners for centuries. First used to aid whalers returning from hunting their game, the lighthouse is a popular tourist attraction today. On the National Register of Historic Places, the structure features antiques and lighthouse memorabilia. Guests can also visit the Lighthouse Cottage and Herb Gardens, which feature more than 200 different plants.

where to eat

Doo-Wop Diner. 4010 Boardwalk, Wildwood; (609) 522-7880. While you'll run across many a tourist at this popular retro diner, it still merits a visit for its distinctive atmosphere and family friendly vibe. The decor is distinctly kitschy, with jukeboxes blasting '50s tunes and employees outfitted in retro-ware. And the food, while not winning any culinary awards, satisfies. Opt for standards such as burgers (the menu lists about 20) or patty melts and you'll be good. Don't leave without trying a milkshake. With flavors like bubble gum, guava, and pumpkin pie, the kid in you will rejoice. $$.

Marie Nicole's. 9510 Pacific Ave., Wildwood Crest; (609) 522-5425. One of the area's best restaurants. Marie Nicole's offers a small but choice selection of appetizers and entrees from tuna tartare to shrimp wontons to wasabi tuna and seafood risotto. The decor is a mix of warm and cool, with cherry wood and white tablecloths situated around the dining room. The award-winning wine list is reasonably priced and showcases mainly California and Italian varietals. $$$.

Maui's Dog House. Eighth and New Jersey Avenues, North Wildwood. You don't have to be Guy Fieri to love Maui's Dog House, which was featured on the Food Network series, *Diners, Drive Ins and Dives.* The small shop lists more than 20 different types of German-style hotdogs (made of pork, beef, and veal). Vegetarians aren't neglected as the shop also serves a small selection of veggie dogs. The shop is not just about dogs. You can also try a burger or a chicken sandwich (six varieties). While many visitors would opt for french fries on the side, you'd be doing a disservice if you didn't try the salty balls. These potato balls are cooked in salt and special spice and dipped in butter for added effect. Yum. $$.

where to stay

Caribbean. 5600 Ocean Ave., Wildwood Crest; (609) 522-8292. Many of the accommodations in town have a Doo Wop theme and Caribbean is the best of the bunch. A motel rather than a hotel, it's not your dirty roadside version. Instead, guests are treated to clean and colorful rooms with an island appeal. Beds are encased in colorful striped bedspreads as palm tree designs hang overhead. Built in 1957, the motel has modern amenities such as flat-screen TVs and free Wi-Fi. There's also a gas grill available for guests' use. Relax at the large moon-shaped outdoor pool or the fun cabana lounge. $.

StarLux. 305 East Rio Grande Ave., Wildwood; (609) 522-7412. A unique boutique hotel on the boardwalk, StarLux offers standard rooms and suites as well as separate houses and trailers. Yes, trailers. Standard rooms are fairly bare bones, with beds, microwaves, and fridges. But the homes are freestanding cottages that are perfect for families. Still it's the trailers that are the reason you stay here. The colorful interior features beds, kitchenettes, and small bathing areas. All rooms have free Wi-Fi. Guests can enjoy the year-round hot tub, community pool, and game room. StarLux affords guests complimentary bicycle usage. Tool around on a Hampton Cruiser. It's the best way to get around the seaside towns. $$.

cape may

Sometimes you want to really get away from the city yet you don't want to give up the comforts of home. What would a day trip be without opportunities to dine in great restaurants or see historic sites? Cape May as a destination offers quiet spaces to relax and admire nature as well as fine dining establishments and enough history to satisfy that buff in your family. Straddling the Delaware Bay at the Atlantic Ocean, the town was named for a Dutch sea captain who discovered the area in 1620 and has since been a destination rich in maritime history. Since the 18th century, city dwellers from Philly and New York have flocked here to flee urban congestion. It's considered the oldest seaside resort in the nation. Although thousands of tourists head here in the summer each year, it never feels overrun, thanks to the way the town is laid out and areas for quiet contemplation. Visitors can bird watch, look for whales, sport fish, or just find a place to sit on the beach and relax. Still, you'll want to hit the myriad dining options, cultural attractions, and summer festivals.

getting there

From Wildwoods, take Wildwood Boulevard to the Garden State Parkway S for 4 miles until you reach NJ 109 S. Continue onto Lafayette Street.

where to go

Cape May Bird Observatory at The Northwood Center. 701 East Lake Dr., Cape May; (609) 884-2736. Cape May is a popular bird-watching destination, and many birders head here throughout the spring and summer. A member of the New Jersey Audubon Society, the observatory hosts bird walks and boat trips as well as education programs for people of all ages. Specialty weekend events occur throughout the year. And if you've forgotten your binoculars at home or are new to the pastime, the observatory sells various accoutrements through its Feather*Edge* optics store.

Cape May Lighthouse. Cape May Point State Park, Lower Township, Cape May. This 157-foot lighthouse is arguably the biggest attraction in the Cape May area. Located at Cape May Point State Park, the 19th-century lighthouse still serves as a beacon for incoming ships. Climb the 217 steps for a spectacular view of the peninsula.

Cape May Stage. At The Robert Shackleton Playhouse, Corner of Bank and Lafayette Streets, Cape May; (609) 884-1341. Since 1988, visitors from around the area have enjoyed the theater productions at Cape May Stage. Housed in a former Presbyterian church, the equity theater company launches numerous plays during the summer, often featuring

Broadway actors and singers. The playhouse is small, with only a 110-person capacity, making it an intimate venue at which to see high-caliber productions such as *The Little Prince* and *Steel Magnolias.* Wheelchair accessible.

Cape May Whale Watch and Research Center. 1286 Wilson Dr., Cape May; (609) 898-0055. Whale watching is a popular pastime on the Eastern seaboard, and the Cape May Whale Watch and Research Center is one of the East Coast's most well-respected sea mammal research facilities in the country. The center tracks the migratory and breeding patterns of dolphins and whales in the area. It also sponsors 2-hour whale and dolphin watching trips. Food and soft drinks are included in the price of admission. In the event that no whales or dolphins are sighted, the organization takes visitors on another trip. Part of the trip proceeds supports research and marine education.

East Lynne Theater Company. 500 Hughes St., Cape May; (609) 884-5898. For more than 30 years, the East Lynne Theater Company has produced 135 plays honoring the American spirit. From plays about early American life such as *Aunt Maddie's House* to stories about notorious Americans such as *Lizzie Borden Live,* the East Lynne Theater offers a unique perspective when it comes to live theater. The company performs at the First Presbyterian Church of Cape May, with seating for 150 people.

Emlen Physick Estate. 1048 Washington St., Cape May; (609) 884-5404. This 18-room Victorian mansion was home to Dr. Emlen Physick, prominent Philadelphia-area physician. The stick style has decorative shingles and Queen Anne details. The Mid-Atlantic Center for the Arts & Humanities saved the estate from the wreaking ball in 1970. Today it's home to the MAC and open for tours inside the mansion as well as the grounds and gardens.

Mid-Atlantic Center for the Arts & Humanities. 1048 Washington St., Cape May; (609) 884-4244. This nonprofit organization promotes and preserves Cape May's unique appeal. Concerned residents started the organization in 1970 to save local landmarks from disrepair and demolition. Today, the group organizes walking and old-fashioned trolley tours of area landmarks as well as celebrations marking significant events in Cape May's history, from Black History Month to treasure hunts to wine weekends.

where to shop

Colors. 518 Washington St., Cape May; (609) 884-0336. Situated on the main shopping drag, Colors is a popular boutique for both men and women as the shop carries several lines of casual and contemporary clothing. Much of the selection is made of natural fibers such as cotton and linen, and you can find a wealth of sizes not just the dreaded size 4. Prices are fairly reasonable and the shop has seasonal sales.

Gail Pierson Gallery. 658 Washington St., Cape May; (609) 884-2585. Gail Pierson is a local artist and gallery owner who hosts events and openings throughout the year and sells contemporary art by Cape May area artists. The space is small but packed with unusual and unique pieces. The Matt Lively paintings are particularly appealing for their whimsical scenes.

A Place on Earth. 526 Washington St., Cape May; (609) 898-0039. Looking for handmade soaps and other sundries? Head to A Place on Earth. The shop makes its own soaps, bath fizzes, herbs, tub teas scrubs, etc. much in the vein of bath product giant, Lush. This is a small, independent store that makes its products in-house and much of it is natural or organic. Olive oil and natural herbs such as rosemary and lavender are used. Prices are a bit steep but you're paying more for carefully crafted gifts.

Seaweeds by the Sea. 315–18 Ocean St., Cape May; (609) 898-9300. A boutique that specializes in women's clothing, hats, jewelry, and handbags, Seaweeds by the Sea is a local stronghold. Many of the brands showcased in the boutique are small marques such as Chamilia, Vera Bradley, and Brighton. Most of the small shop's selection is brightly colored and whimsical, with natural fibers getting the most play. Prices are pretty fair considering the location.

where to eat

Black Duck on Sunset. 1 Sunset Blvd., Cape May; (609) 898-0100. This BYOB bistro serves up some of the heartiest food in town. Housed in a clapboard home, the Black Duck boasts a menu replete in local seafood. Try the jumbo lump crab cakes or the grouper in potato crust. Some of the items have an Asian tinge to them even though the food is Napa-inspired. The ambience is elegant without being pretentious or stuffy. $$$.

Dellas 5 & 10 Soda Fountain. 501–503 Washington St., Cape May; (609) 884-4568. A local institution since 1947, Dellas 5 & 10 Soda Fountain has drawn locals and tourists alike for its unpretentious ice-cream floats, egg creams, sandwiches, and other items from the golden days. The decor is kitschy. It's as if you've stepped into 1950s America. But Dellas isn't jumping on a retro bandwagon. This has always been the restaurant's style. Dellas also doubles as a sundry store. $$.

410 Bank Street. 410 Bank St., Cape May; (609) 884-2127. This award-winning restaurant is often on "Best of New Jersey" lists. Why? Because it serves authentic Creole dishes. Housed in a 19th-century carriage house, 410 Bank Street offers elegantly appointed indoor and outdoor seating. Sit among hanging fronds. Chef Henry Sing Cheng is a virtuoso in the kitchen, crafting innovative seafood dishes such as scallops in a Creole broth and blackened ribs with corn chili. $$$.

Lobster House. 906 Schellengers Landing Rd., Cape May; (609) 884-8296. A long and established restaurant in Cape May, the Lobster House serves locally sourced seafood and fish in a casual setting. You won't find pretension here. What you will find is high quality food served with a smile. Checkered tablecloths envelope wooden tables. The restaurant offers a great view of the harbor. Try something from the raw bar or the famous clam soup. Don't skip on any main courses. Portions are generous and everything tastes as if it was just caught. Opt for the charbroiled fresh fish or two-pound lobster. There is also a small kids' menu. $$$.

where to stay

Cape May offers a wealth of accommodations, from small bed-and-breakfasts to historic manses to motels. While it's hard to pick the best, Congress Hall and The Virginia Hotel stand out.

Congress Hall. 251 Beach Ave., Cape May; (888) 944-1816. What started out as a boarding house has become one of Cape May's most majestic and popular hotels. Since 1816, guests have been treated like kings at Congress Hall (albeit, except for those times when it was in disrepair or had burned down). The current structure served as a Bible education site for many years. It was renovated in 1995 to its original elegant standards. The wrap-around porch has views of both land and sea. Rooms are colorful yet elegant with marble. Guests are treated to many luxurious amenities, including Belgian cotton sheets, a full-service spa, private beach cabanas, and a nightclub and cocktail lounge. The Blue Pig Tavern serves low-key comfort food, and The Brown Room cocktail lounge is a casual place to unwind. $$$$.

The Virginia Hotel. 25 Jackson St., Cape May; (800) 732-4236. This historic boutique hotel offers a unique experience. It mixes the best qualities of a bed-and-breakfast with a larger, luxury hotel. Each of the 24 cozy rooms has floral wallpaper, sunburst mirrors, and creative artwork. Italian and Belgian cotton linens envelope comfortable, expansive beds that you can sink into. Bathrooms are large and homey with Bulgari products. If you don't want to stay with other guests, opt for one of the five unique cottages, each with its own color scheme and design aesthetic. The cottages serve as your home away from home as they are equipped with kitchens and dining areas. $$$.

east

day trip 01

east

long island wineries:
mattituck, new york
southold, new york

Wine has been a Long Island staple since 1973, when Alex and Louisa Hargrave planted the first vines in the area. Today, it's one of the biggest draws to the island's North Fork, where 30 wineries abound. The fertile land has a rich and varied agricultural history; it was once used for potato farming. Much of that land has been converted to winemaking. Although Cutchogue and Peconic have more wineries per capita, the seaside towns of Mattituck and Southold are of particular note due to their award-winning wineries, eateries, and high-end lodging.

mattituck

Once a Corchaug Indian stronghold, Mattituck has been a sleepy hamlet since the late 1700s when English farmers settled the area. Quiet tree-lined streets abut duney beaches and inlets as the town borders both the Long Island Sound and the Great Peconic Bay. A drive here takes you past farm stands selling organic produce and verdant vineyards aplenty. The site of the Mattituck Yacht Club as you make your way into town makes any landlubber wish for a seafaring friend.

getting there

Take the Queens Midtown Expressway to I-495 E to Long Island. Exit onto NY 25 E toward Riverhead. Turn right at Main Road. The trip takes an hour and 38 minutes, without traffic.

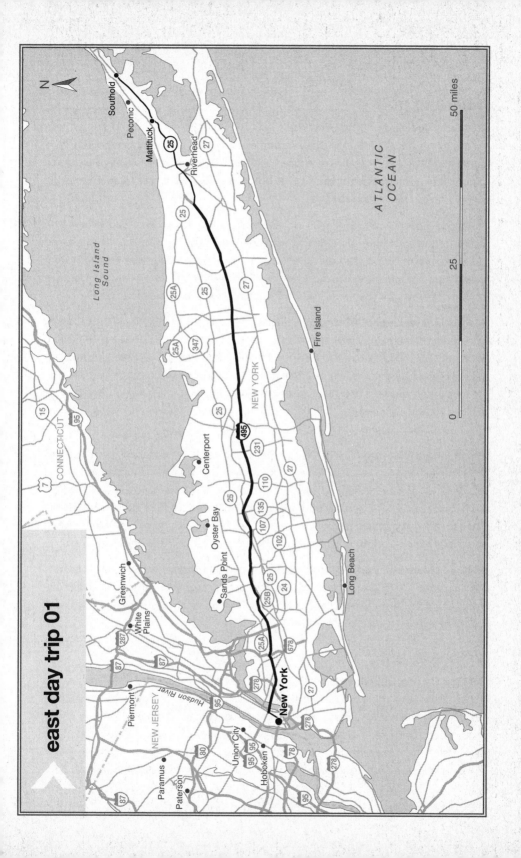

east day trip 01

where to go

Gramercy Vineyards. 10020 South Ave., Mattituck; (631) 298-1213. Travelers would pass by this diminutive winery if they didn't know it existed. What Gramercy Vineyards lacks in size it makes up for in depth. The Estate Merlot and Reserve Estate Merlot pack a taste wallop. The 3½-acre estate produces three boutique wines, which are only available at the winery's tasting room in nearby Peconic.

Highwind Farm. 1150 Old Main Rd., Mattituck; (631) 298-4341. This 60-acre horse farm boards as well as sells horses. Owners Susan Lomangino and Tom Yovino offer year-round dressage, hunter-jumper, and reining lessons for expert riders. Beginners will benefit from carefully guided riding lessons and children will enjoy the pony rides. The farm boasts a heated indoor ring for riders wanting to enjoy the pastime in cold weather months.

Macari Vineyards and Winery. 150 Bergen Ave., Mattituck; (631) 298-0100. Owners Joseph and Katherine Macari and their son Joseph Jr. established this 180-acre waterfront winery in 1995 although the family owned the 500-acre estate for 50 years. The Macaris believe in preserving the environment so much of their winemaking has an organic feel to it. The vineyard is known for its stellar white wines, most notably its Sauvignon Blanc, Chardonnay, Viognier, and Riesling. The estate also has compost fields and farmland for cows, goats, and Sicilian donkeys to graze.

Shinn Estate Vineyards. 2000 Oregon Rd., Mattituck; (631) 804-0367. Shinn Estates is often cited as the best of all North Fork wineries, and tasting the Wild Board Doe (a Bordeaux-style wine) you have no reason to dispute that claim. The winery is small by North Fork standards, only 20 acres in all, making it easier for owners Barbara Shinn and David Page to make biodynamic wine. The tasting room is open seven days a week with walking tours available on weekends. Shinn Estate also runs a small bed-and-breakfast on-site.

Veterans Memorial Park. Mattituck. Situated on Great Peconic bay, this lovely park and beach has a bocce court, shuffleboard, and horseshoe pitch onsite. Families wanting to picnic or barbecue can at the west end of the park. The park also has a fenced-in playground complete with swings and monkey bars.

where to eat

A Mano Osteria and Wine Bar. 13550 Main Rd., Mattituck; (631) 298-4800. A cozy and casual Italian eatery that focuses on fresh food and bold Tuscan flavors. A Mano offers affordable fare in a lovely setting overlooking a flower garden. The menu is big on homemade pizza (the dinner selection has seven different varieties), Italian cheeses, and meats and pasta. The restaurant even offers gluten-free options. The restaurant hosts special events and frequent wine dinners that focus on local wines as well as Italian varietals. $$.

Love Lane Kitchen. 240 Love Lane, Mattituck; (631) 298-8989. Love Lane Kitchen is a local favorite as much for its homey atmosphere as for its affordable menu. The fare, featuring Mediterranean and American staples, is all locally sourced and homemade and changes regularly. Recent highlights included a butterhead lettuce appetizer with blue cheese fondue and Moroccan-style duck tagine. The restaurant hosts wine and beer dinners, pairing local wines and beers with its artfully crafted food. $$.

The Village Cheese Shop North. 105 Love Lane, Mattituck; (631) 298-8556. This fromagerie-cum-bar can't be missed. The Village Cheese Shop boasts an impressive selection of cheeses from around the world, including France, Italy, England, Argentina, and Holland. The shop sells cured meats and wine as well. Relax at the small cheese bar and savor the creamy fondue or Swiss raclette. $$.

where to stay

Cedar House on Sound B&B. 4850 Sound Ave., Mattituck; (631) 298-7676. Opened in 2010, the Cedar House on Sound B&B takes preserving the environment seriously. At the end of 2010, the hotel installed 45 solar panels to cut electricity costs. The expansive property includes several barns that were once part of a dairy farm. The main house was a potato-packing barn and now includes 5 rooms all with wrought iron beds, Egyptian cotton sheets, flatscreen TVs, and Wi-Fi access. Courtyard rooms are neutral in color and overlook the barns. The large vineyard suites are decorated in rich reds and overlook the small vineyards on the property. $$$.

Shinn Estate Farmhouse. 2000 Oregon Rd., Mattituck; (631) 804-0367. Shinn Estate Vineyards plays hosts to overnight guests at their on-site bed-and-breakfast. The 1880 homestead offers a pleasing respite for city folks. The private rooms have hardwood floors, en suite bathrooms, and gorgeous views of the vineyards. Enjoy a glass of rosé as you sit on the large front porch. $$$.

southold

Larger and more cosmopolitan than Mattituck, Southold boasts more wineries than almost any other town in the North Folk (only Cutchogue and Peconic have it beat). The hamlet was first settled in 1640 by English puritans and grew quickly. (The town had only 180 citizens in 1650. Fifty years later, that number had increased tenfold.) Today, more than 20,000 people call the town home, and although it's teeming with restaurants and farm stands in addition to the wineries, locals have remained friendly and helpful.

getting there

From Mattituck, take the Main Road (NY 25) 8 miles north to Southold. It's about a 9-minute drive, barring traffic, which is heavy in summer.

where to go

Corey Creek Vineyards. 45470 Main Rd./NY 25, Southold; (631) 765-4168. Part of the Bedell Cellars family, Corey Creek Vineyards is a 23-acre estate that mainly produces Chardonnay, Merlot, and Cabernet Franc (its Chardonnay and Gewürztraminer often win tasting contests). The tasting room and gift shop are housed in a wooden barnlike structure. Visitors have breathtaking views of the vineyards and beyond.

Croteaux Vineyards. 1450 South Harbour Rd., Southold; (631) 765-6099. Known primarily for rosé, Croteaux Vineyards occupies the land of two historic North Fork Farms—the 18th-century Howell Farm and the mid-19th-century Stepnoski Farm. The historic buildings were lovingly restored when Paula Croteau purchased the properties in the early 1990s. The 10.5-acre vineyards have existed since 2003, and include cloned Merlot, Cabernet Franc, and Sauvignon Blanc.

Duck Walk North. 44535 Main Rd./NY 25, Southold; (631) 765-3500. The sister property of Southampton's Duck Walk South, this 30-acre winery is known for its crisp and fruity Sauvignon Blanc. The vineyard is environmentally friendly, using geothermal energy for heating and cooling and well water to replenish the soil.

Old Field Vineyards. 59600 Main Rd./NY 25, Southold; (631) 765-0004. Family-owned and -operated for several generations, Old Field Vineyards was once a potato and cauliflower farm before being transformed into a working winery by owner Chris Baiz. Baiz grew fruit on the land from the early 1970s until the mid-1990s. The vineyards' first vintage was a 1997 Pinot Noir. Today, Old Field is known for its Merlot, Cabernet Franc, Chardonnay, Blush de Noir, and Blanc de Noir sparkling wine. Baiz conducts hour-and-a-half-long tours of the property including the ice house and old tavern building.

One Woman Vineyards. 5195 Old North Rd., Southold; (631) 765-1200. As the name suggests, this vineyard is the brainchild of one woman, Italian Claudia Purita. Purita tends to 10 acres of vineyard and farmland and produces just a small amount of white wine and rosé. The Reserve Chardonnay and Gewürztraminer are particularly delicious. Old Woman wines can be found at New York City's BLT Steak, the Four Seasons, and the Waldorf Astoria.

Sparkling Pointe Vineyards. 39750 CR 48, Southold; (631) 765-0200. If you love sparkling wine, head to this 29-acre vineyard that specializes in bubbly. The vineyard produces Brut, Blanc de Blancs, as well as two other wines called Topaz Imperial and Brut Seduction. The main house is styled like a nouveau French country manor and can be booked for private events and weddings year-round.

where to eat

Jeni's Main Street Grill. 54195 Main Rd./NY 25, Southold; (631) 765-9610. Known mainly as a breakfast joint, Jeni's Main Street Grill also serves delicious lunch fare. Owner Jennifer Raymond serves hearty country fare in a relaxed homey setting. A counter displays homemade baked goods. Customers can order from a seasonal menu with the ubiquitous breakfast items (eggs Benedict, breakfast burrito) as well as specialty fare such as pumpkin cinnamon rolls, French toast, and sweet potato pancakes. Raymond also teaches cooking classes. $$.

North Fork Table & Inn. 57225 Main Rd./NY 25, Southold; (631) 765-0177. Seasonally-inspired and locally-grown fare garner top billing at this award-winning North Fork icon. The atmosphere is more formal than other area restaurants. White tablecloths and apron-clad servers abound. North Fork Table's menu features a diverse selection of organic and locally sourced dishes, from Block Island fluke to Long Island duck. Guests have a choice of a $68, 3-course prix fixe menu or the chef's tasting menu (children under 12 are offered a 2-course prix fixe menu). The menu changes frequently due to the availability of local produce and meats. Closed Tues and Wed. $$$.

Southold Fish Market. 61850 Main Rd./NY 25, Southold; (631) 765-3200. If you're in the mood for fresh seafood, head to this iconic fish market and take-out joint on Route 25. Owner Charlie Manwaring sells fresh local seafood such as bay scallops, clams, and lobster. The shop doubles as a takeaway. The extensive menu lists soups, quesadillas, steamed seafood, and fried and grilled wraps and entrees. The prices are decent especially for a popular destination such as Southold. $$.

where to stay

North Fork Inn. 57225 Main Rd./NY 25, Southold; (631) 765-0177. Attached to the award-winning North Fork Table, the North Fork Inn feels less like a bed-and-breakfast and more like a European boutique hotel. The inn has four cozy accommodations, all elegantly appointed with luxurious amenities including sleigh beds, Frette linens, locally sourced bath products, private climate controls, and flat screen TVs. Breakfast is served at the North Fork table. $$$.

Shorecrest Bed-and-Breakfast. 54300 CR 48, Southold; (631) 765-1570. On a bluff overlooking the Long Island Sound, Shorecrest offers seven distinctive accommodations. Six of the rooms are housed in the shingled main manse and are designed to reflect different regions and themes. Choose from the European country charm of the French Provençal-style West Room to the Oriental-theme Silk Road Room. The family friendly, 3-bedroom Shorecrest Beach House overlooks a private beach. Guests of the beach house have to pay extra for breakfast. $$$.

Willow Hill House Bed-and-Breakfast. 48850 Main Rd./NY 25, Southold; (631) 765-1575. Once home to a whaling ship captain, the Victorian Willow Hill House now serves as homey accommodations for city dwellers looking for a comfortable inn to rest their weary heads. The 3 rooms all feature period antiques, full beds, and kitschy quilts and linens. The 2 rooms on the top floor share a bathroom, the third room shares a bath with the innkeepers. $$$.

worth more time

Although the town of **Greenport,** at the end of the North Fork near Orient and Gardiners Bay, isn't included in this guide (it's more than 2 hours by car from New York City), it's a not-to-be-missed stop for anyone wanting to extend their stay in the area. Once a major whaling port, Greenport is now a sailing mecca, with sailboats lining the slips of the town's five marinas from May to Sept. **The Morning Glory** (www.themorningglory.com) is a 19th-century bed-and-breakfast in town, and its decor is decidedly un-kitschy. You won't find your grandmother's old afghan here. Owners Klaus and Renate Wilhelm are environmentally conscious, utilizing organic produce and natural cleaning supplies and providing guests with filtered water in glass bottles.

day trip 02

east

>>>

beachcombing:
long beach, new york
fire island, new york

New Yorkers lament the lack of good beaches in the city. Taking the subway to Coney Island and the Rockaways means coming across the types of vagrants that you escape to the beach to get *away* from. Thankfully, two lovely beaches, located on separate islands, are less than 2 hours away. Long Beach is a middle-class town with a plethora of restaurants and bars, a wooden, 2¼-mile boardwalk, and a clean, white-sand beach. Fire Island is the birthplace of disco and is a tony gay-friendly enclave that's home to a number of quaint eateries and bars but is known more as a relaxing weekend getaway.

long beach

Long Beach began as a resort community in 1882 when the Long Island Railroad was built. The small barrier island, on the south end of larger Long Island, grew steadily as more city dwellers discovered its many delights. In 1912, the 2¼-mile boardwalk was built, with the help of elephants. It went through a decline in the 1970s and '80s when people abandoned the resort for tonier communities further east. Seaside retirement centers popped up, and drug dealers and junkies took over the beach. Thankfully, things turned around in the 1990s. Today, it's a popular suburb and summer retreat for city dwellers. The retirement homes have been transformed into luxury condos. Surfers and bikers flock here for the great waves and bike lane on the boardwalk, respectively.

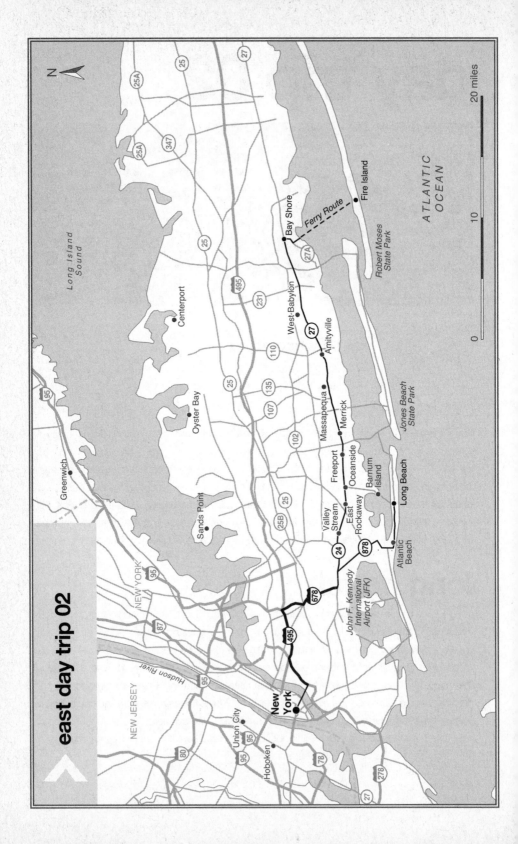

^ east day trip 02

getting there

The Long Island Railroad runs regular trains from New York's Penn Station to Long Beach throughout the peak summer months. The trip to Long Beach takes about 55 minutes. Weekdays are always better than weekends, when you'll be jostling for space with other city dwellers. The center of Long Beach is 2 blocks from the train station; the beach a mere 7 blocks away.

If you'd rather drive, the route is an easy and short one (about 45 minutes to an hour, depending on traffic). Take the Queens Midtown Expressway to I-495 to the Long Island Expressway. Connect to I-678 S/Van Wyck Expressway. Continue onto the Nassau Expressway/NY 878 W. Because it's a barrier island, you'll have to cross the Atlantic Beach Bridge to get there. This is a toll road so have cash handy. Continue east on Beech Street past Atlantic Beach to Long Beach.

where to go

The Beach. With more than 3½ miles of white sand, the beach is the biggest attraction in Long Beach. During the summer, it's hard to find open space, especially if you stick close to the train station. Head one mile west or east for open space. Teenage lifeguards are on duty daily from July 4 through Labor Day and they take their job seriously. Just try to take your boogie board in the water without fins. You'll be summarily dragged out of the water and reprimanded for not following the rules. Alcoholic beverages are not permitted on the beach. (While nothing beats sitting on a lifeguard chair and watching the sunset as you sip a bottle of wine, rules are rules.)

Long Beach Historical Museum. 226 West Penn St.; (516) 432-1192. Housed in a century-old, 2-story, Craftsman-style, white stucco home, the Long Beach Historical Museum preserves artifacts from the seaside town's past. The museum has been restored, with period-esque furnishings. The second story houses the museum's archives, and the backyard features an original boardwalk bench and a pergola floor made of bricks from the city's past.

where to shop

Buddy's Bikes. 907 West Beech St., Long Beach; (516) 431-0804. Long Beach is a haven for cyclists. You'll find hundreds of people riding their bicycles to and from the beach during the summer months. Naturally, there are a plethora of bike stores in town. Buddy's Bikes is the friendliest of the bunch. The store has a good selection of colorful Hampton Cruisers for sale and rent. And if your bike breaks down, the helpful staff will quickly repair it for you.

unsOund Surf Shop. 359 East Park Ave., Long Beach; (516) 889-1112. Unlike other surf shops on Long Island, unsOund provides friendly service, regardless of your level of expertise or your gender. The 14-year-old shop was formed by two locals surfers who test all products sold in the store. Boards are reasonably priced and all the major brands are represented—Cole, WRV, Lost, etc. The store sells skateboard and snowboard equipment and accessories as well. If you're a casual surfing, unsOund also rents boards.

where to eat

Molly's Fish Market. 958 West Beech St., Long Beach; (516) 432-1051. Long Beach has quite a few seafood restaurants but Molly's Fish Market is by far the best and the most affordable. The space doubles as a fish market but guests can order from a wide selection of fresh fish, seafood, and soup. The Alaskan king crabs, oysters, scallops, and lobster bisque are delicious. If you're still hungry, you can take home something to cook on your grill. $$.

Nagahama. 169 East Park Ave., Long Beach; (516) 432-6446. The only sushi spot in town, Nagahama serves a variety of fresh sushi, sashimi, and other signature dishes. The gyoza and shumai are particularly appetizing. The place is hopping, with a 20- to 30-minute wait on Fri and Sat nights. Service is attentive and friendly. You never feel rushed into leaving. $$.

Speakeasy. 1032 West Beech St., Long Beach; (516) 889-3279. Unlike many of the bars lining Beech Street, you can actually have a conversation and hear it all at Speakeasy. Getting a drink isn't difficult either. The food is typical bar fare—burgers and seafood entrees get top billing—but is atypically fresh. This is the place to go if you're a sports lover wanting to watch the game without loudmouth frat boys as acoustic companions. Local musicians perform during the summer. $$.

where to stay

Allegria Hotel. 80 West Broadway, Long Beach; (516) 889-1300. The only lodging in town, the Allegria is a Manhattan-style luxury hotel that offers amazing views of the ocean and busy boardwalk. The 143 rooms and suites all have sea views. Rooms and suites are modern and outfitted with Egyptian cotton sheets, limestone baths, and flat screen TVs. The design is beach chic, with neutrals and pops of blue on beds and chairs. The hotel has a private beach tunnel that allows access to the white sand and lounge chairs. The hotel also provides surfboard instruction and rental. $$$.

fire island

What was once a whaling station is now one of the chicest beaches on Long Island. Fire Island has a history of welcoming visitors. Its lighthouse was one of the first things immigrants saw when arriving in America during the late 19th and early 20th century. While remnants of its whaling past remain, the barrier island, which abuts the south shore of Long Island, is now dotted with beach bungalows and elegant colonial-style summer homes.

New Yorkers beat the summer heat and head here on weekends to soak in the rays, dig for clams, hike, bike, fish, surf, or just enjoy backyard BBQs. In recent decades, it has seen an influx of gay and lesbian residents who have made it a welcoming retreat for anyone who frequents an alternative lifestyle. Don't be shocked to see fully nude sunbathers on the beach. Bring your bike or be prepared to walk. As well as being carefree, the island is completely car-free.

getting there

To hit both spots in one day, travelers need to backtrack from Long Beach and transfer to a Fire Island–bound train. The journey is long and a little tricky. From Long Beach, take the Long Island Rail Road to Jamaica (25 minutes) and transfer to a Ronkonkoma-bound train. Get off the train at Sayville (1 hour) and take a short taxi ride to the Sayville Ferry terminal at 41 River Rd. Ferries run every hour during summer weekends. It's about a 30-minute ride. Fire Island ferries drop you in either the male-centric Pines or the female-centric Cherry Grove.

Fire Island doesn't allow cars so you won't be able to go all the way onto the barrier island with your wheels. Still, you can get close enough and then transfer to the ferry. From Long Beach head east on Park Avenue towards Lido Boulevard to Loop Parkway. The Loop Parkway will connect with the Meadowbrook State Parkway North. Connect to Sunrise Highway/NY 27 E through Merrick. Continue on Sunrise Highway until you get near Bay Shore. Take a right on Brentwood Road and a left on NY 27A. Head down Main Street and take a left on Maple Avenue. That will lead you to the Bay Shore–Fire Island Ferry Terminal. Park your car and hop on the ferry. It's an hour drive.

where to go

Fire Island Lighthouse. A must-see for anyone interested in the island's seafaring history. The Fire Island Lighthouse was built in 1857 and was a beacon of hope for 19th- and 20th-century European immigrants. The Fire Island Lighthouse Preservation Society recently restored the lighthouse and is now offering guided tours to the observatory. Gaze in wonder at the view off Long Island, the Atlantic Ocean, the Great South Bay, and Fire Island beaches. If you squint, you can even see part of the Manhattan skyline.

Fire Island National Seashore. Oh, if Lyndon Johnson could see it now. In 1964, the former president signed the bill making the seashore a national treasure. Even though it's overrun in the summer with city dwellers looking for an unpretentious alternative to the Hamptons, everyone treats it with respect. The 101-mile pristine beach offers hypnotic waves, high dunes, and plentiful wildlife. If you want to get away from it all, you can, even if the Pines and Cherry Grove areas are bustling. On the more tranquil sections of beach you may have to toss a crab shell or two back in the ocean. Never fear. You'll return to less arduous pursuits in seconds. The beach is a haven for surfers, sailors, clam diggers, and fisherman.

Sunken Forest at Sailors Haven. Said to be below sea level, the Sunken Forest is one of the last maritime woodlands on the east coast. This 40-acre refuge is a must for hikers, birders, and horticulturalists. Walk through fields of blueberry, sassafras, and misshapen 200-year-old trees. Guided tours through the boardwalk trail are available during the summer.

where to eat

Bocce Beach. 927 Evergreen Walk, Ocean Beach; (631) 583-8100. Situated on Ocean Beach on the north side of the island, this restaurant and bar serves fresh seafood and meat dishes in a casual setting. The restaurant hosts rib night on Wednesday and Sunday and guests can opt for the prix fixe, 3-course Taste of Fire Island. A good selection of domestic and imported beers are available as well as wine. Unlike the name suggests, no indoor bocce court exists. $$.

CJ's Allegro. 479 Bay Walk, Ocean Beach; (631) 583-9890. Open year-round this casual Ocean Beach bar/restaurant is a relaxed place in the off-season but is swarming with locals and tourists during the summer. Head here on the early side if you want a seat and to dine. The food is standard bar grub but the drinks are unusual and potent. $$.

where to stay

Dune Point. 134 Lewis Walk, Cherry Grove; (631) 597-6261. This condo-style hotel caters to a sophisticated crowd. Most of the self-catering apartments and studios have decks and ocean views. The decor is decidedly neutral with modern fixtures and furnishings. All rooms have small kitchens that come equipped with the essentials (stove, oven, fridge, etc.). The hotel has BBQs for guests' use as well as chaise lounges and gazebos. The hotel offers 20 percent discounts for week stays. $$$.

Madison Fire Island Pines. 22 Island Walk, Fire Island Pines; (631) 597-6061. Just a minute's walk from the ferry is this small boutique hotel that has an airy Caribbean feel. Guests have the choice of three accommodations—Madison Rooms, Garden Rooms, and Penthouse Rooms. The first two are fairly standard—the second being the more exclusive of the two—but the third are equipped with glass walls that overlook a pool deck as well as high ceilings and private terraces. Guests have access to a swimming pool and pool deck as well as a roof deck. $$$.

day trip 03

east

gold coast treasures:
centerport, new york
old westbury, new york
sands point, new york

Although New York City has long been home to some of the wealthiest residents in the country, many old money families built estates outside of the city. Certain sections of Long Island have long been synonymous with American royalty. Many of New York City's elite built mansions on the so-called Gold Coast, which is on the island's north shore. The wealthy wanted to get away from the hoi polloi and entertain with others of a similar stature and importance. Three towns in particular are worthy of examination: Centerport, Old Westbury, and Sands Point. All have a history of welcoming the uber-rich. To this day, they are enclaves for the prosperous, and if you can't get to Newport, Rhode Island, this is the next best thing to seeing stately old mansions.

centerport

The easternmost hamlet on the storied Gold Coast, Centerport has the enviable position of being the most beautiful of all Gold Coast towns. Part of that has to do with its location on a peninsula abutting Northport Harbor and Centerport Harbor. Get ready for warm summer breezes and bougainvillea blooming profusely. It also has to do with the stately homes scattered throughout the town. The most noteworthy of these is the Vanderbilt Estate, which encompasses 43 acres overlooking Northport Harbor. If you start this day trip here, you may never make it to the next two towns.

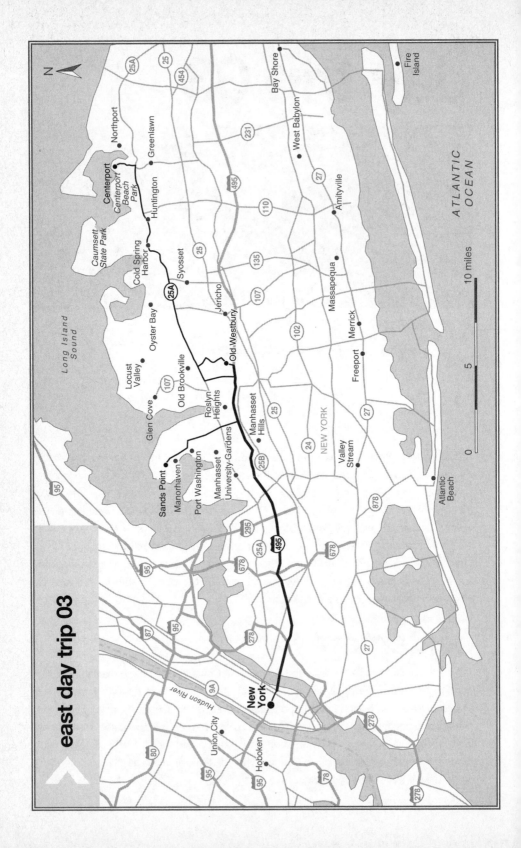

east day trip 03

getting there

Take the Queens Midtown Tunnel to the Queens Midtown Expressway/I-495. It turns into the Long Island Expressway. Merge onto Nassau Boulevard, turn left at Searington Road and turn right at NY 25A E. Take a left at Little Neck Road. The trip takes about an hour, barring traffic.

where to go

Suffolk County Vanderbilt Museum. 180 Little Neck Rd., Centerport; (631) 854-5555. Once home to William K. Vanderbilt II (patriarch Cornelius's great-grandson), the Vanderbilt homestead, aka Eagles Nest, has been a museum since 1950 per Vanderbilt's will. Built over the course of three decades (1910–36), the 24-room home is a grand mansion, built in the Spanish Revival style, which was unusual at the time. Rooms are filled with antiques, vintage paintings, and sculpture. The expansive property also features a marine museum, curator's cottage, airplane hanger, boathouse, gardens, and fountains. Vanderbilt was a natural history buff, and much of the land reflects this. Suffolk County built a planetarium on the premises in 1970. Living history guided tours are available throughout the summer.

where to eat

Mill Pond Restaurant. 437 East Main St., Centerport; (631) 261-7663. With spectacular views of the boat basin and even more spectacular steaks, Mill Pond Restaurant easily

the sultan of centerport

Vanderbilt heir William Kissam Vanderbilt built the regal Eagles Nest estate (now the Vanderbilt Museum) in Centerport as a bachelor's retreat. The twice-married Vanderbilt was an automobile and yachting enthusiast, speeding around Long Island via both modes of transport. He was instrumental in creating the Long Island Motor Parkway, one of the earliest paved motorways in the country. Tragically and ironically, his lone son and heir died in an automobile accident in 1933 while heading home from the family's Fisher Island estate. The grief-stricken elder Vanderbilt built an additional wing to his already expansive mansion that housed many of his son's trophies and souvenirs from his travels. William Kissam Vanderbilt died in 1944 of heart failure and bequeathed Eagles Nest to Suffolk County. Today it's one of the biggest draws in all of Long Island.

deserves the raves. The elegant eatery is worth the splurge especially for the sushi, raw seafood, as well as choice seafood and meat dishes. The friendly and knowledgeable wait staff serve juicy steaks, which can be grilled au poivre or Cajun style. $$$.

where to stay

Chalet Inn and Suites. 23 Centershore Rd., Centerport; (631) 757-4600. Centerport doesn't have much to offer in terms of lodging. The Chalet Inn and Suites, the lone hotel in town, won't win any design awards but it's comfortable and clean. Rooms are decorated in traditional hotel decor with floral bedspreads and dark wood furniture. The Chalet Inn stands out from other motels in that it has suites in addition to standard rooms. Suites have ample living and dining space as well as a small kitchen with a fridge. The hotel doesn't offer any amenities except for complimentary breakfast. One hopes that will change when the hotel expands to a larger property across the street (complete with swimming pool and restaurant). $.

old westbury

Old money and new money. They have both made Old Westbury home. What was once a quiet Quaker community turned into an elite playground for wealthy Manhattanites in search of flat countryside on which to hunt foxes and play polo. While not technically on the Gold Coast, Old Westbury has been one of the wealthiest of all New York City suburbs for years (it's the 10th toniest zip code in the country) and was home to a number of grand estates, including Old Westbury Gardens, Spring Hill, Weatley, Erchless, Longfields, and the A. Conger Goodyear House. Unfortunately for visitors and architecture buffs, many of these stately mansions are in ruins today or have been split or torn down to make way for subdivisions.

getting there

It's a 30-minute drive (in good traffic) from Centerport to Old Westbury. Go west on NY 25A until you get to Whitney Lane. Hang a left and you're there.

where to go

Erchless. The Phipps family basically ruled Old Westbury at one point. Besides Old Westbury Gardens, they owned Spring Hill and Erchless. Erchless is one of the few still standing, thanks to the members of the Phipps family who still reside there. Built for Henry's youngest son, Howard, this stately Georgian mansion was built in 1935. The grounds feature gardens, a pond, birch trees, stables, cottages, a greenhouse, koi fountain, and two fantastic Japanese teahouses. The home isn't open to the public but the owners open it from time to time for garden tours.

Old Westbury Gardens. 71 Old Westbury Rd.; (516) 333-0048. Completed in 1906, this is the former estate of John S. and Margarita Grace Phipps. Phipps's father, Henry, was a noted steel magnate and philanthropist. Westbury House, the Charles II–style mansion, sits on 200 verdant acres and is furnished with antiques and artwork from the family vault. Formal gardens, forests, ponds, and lakes make up much of the estate. It's also home to Orchard Hill, the Peggie Phipps Boegner residence that is now used for private functions. The museum hosts guided tours as well as concerts, car shows, horticultural and agricultural events, and lectures.

where to stay

Roslyn Claremont Hotel. 1221 Old Northern Blvd., Roslyn. Old Westbury has few if any lodgings but the nearby village of Roslyn, on route to the next day trip stop of Sands Point, has the Roslyn Claremont Hotel. The 20-year-old property has 76 well-appointed guest rooms. Think bed-and-breakfast rather than chain hotel. Every room has colorful furnishings including chintz curtains and imported bed linens. Guests can choose from smallish twin-bed rooms to roomy suites, some of which have fireplaces and four-poster beds. The hotel has a fitness center as well as Christina's restaurant. $$.

sands point

With no commercial businesses and a reputation as the toniest of all Long Island communities (real estate prices are higher than even The Hamptons), Sands Point has managed to retain much of its grandeur even with developments running roughshod over the land. The town was originally home to three wealthy families: the Sands, the Vanderbilts, and the Cornwells. Writer F. Scott Fitzgerald based part of *The Great Gatsby* here (Daisy Buchanan's family was said to live in Sands Point). In 1917, American industrialist Daniel Guggenheim bought the expansive Castle Gould and Hempstead House estate from fellow tycoon Jay Gould's son Howard. Guggenheim made it the town's focal point, and driving into Sands Point today, you can't miss the blue-capped turrets.

getting there

Take Old Westbury Road to I-495 W to exit 36/Searingtown Road. Take Searingtown Road to Port Washington Boulevard. Take a left on Main Street. Take a right onto Shore Road. The trip takes about 21 minutes in low season.

where to go

Sands Point Preserve. (516) 571-7900. Home to Castle Gould, Hempstead House, and Falaise, this 216-acre preserve was bequeathed to Nassau County by the Guggenheim estate in 1971. Castle Gould should be the first stop. It was erected by Henry Gould in

surf and turf

I have been visiting Long Beach on summer weekends for many years now, partly due to its proximity to New York City and partly due to its relative lack of city beachgoers. It's been nice having a wide swath of white sand to myself. Unfortunately that has changed in the last two years as more Manhattanites discover this gem of a town and its clean beach and lovely boardwalk. Still, there are few better options for a quick trip to the beach as the Hamptons are too snooty and Coney Island is just disgusting.

For years, I didn't give much thought to the surfers wading in the water. One, there didn't seem to be gigantic waves and two, I've seen great surfing in Australia, New Zealand, and Hawaii and didn't think Long Islanders could compete. Boy was I wrong.

In the summer of 2009, two hurricanes passed near Long Island to create massive waves (about 9 feet . . . yeah, massive by New York standards) on the seashore. My friend and I got the great idea to sit on a lifeguard chair and watch the antics of 50 surfers, two of whom were female, compete with each other for choice waves. Impressive aerial derring-do's and somersaults proved to me that Long Island surfers can compete with the best of them.

Long Beach now has a surfing competition, thanks to local aficionados, some of who start at the age of 7. If you know a storm is coming but bypassing the island altogether, bring a beach blanket, relax with your friends and enjoy the spectacle.

1904 to mimic Kilkenny Castle in Ireland. He sold the building and the surrounding acres to Daniel Guggenheim after World War I. Guggenheim loved the old turrets but his wife wasn't a fan so he built nearby Hempstead House for her. The English manor-style home housed medieval tapestries, an aviary, stained glass windows, and artwork by Rembrandt and Rubens. Falaise was home to Daniel's son, Harry. The Norman-style estate boasts a cobblestone courtyard, tiled roofs, carved stone mantels, and 16th- and 17th-century antiques. The preserve is also home to a number of hiking and walking trails that take you through dense forests, ponds, and to the shoreline. The estate hosts medieval reenactments during September.

west

day trip 01

west

the bridges of hunterdon county:
clinton, new jersey
flemington, new jersey

Hunterdon County, New Jersey, isn't a familiar destination for many New Yorkers. They don't like to venture too far into the Garden State for fear of being tainted. That's too bad because they're missing out on several special towns. Hunterdon County has the largest number of truss and stone bridges in the United States. You could spend a day traveling from one to the next. But stop and stay a while in the charming villages of Clinton and Flemington. It's as if a Norman Rockwell painting has come to life. The towns are idyllic, with narrow streets, charming shops and restaurants, historic mills, and a slower pace of life.

clinton

Originally known as Hunts Mills, the town changed its name to Clinton in 1828 to honor Governor Dewitt Clinton, sponsor of the Erie Canal. Although the town dates back to the 1700s, many of the homes in the charming downtown are Victorian. A fire burned the entire village to the ground in 1891. The area is popular for hot air ballooning as well as fruit picking. The center of town features a small waterfall at which geese frolic near red canoes.

getting there

This is an hour-long journey in the best of times but will probably take you an additional 40 minutes. Head west on NJ 495 until you see the signs for NJ 3W. Continue on US 46W.

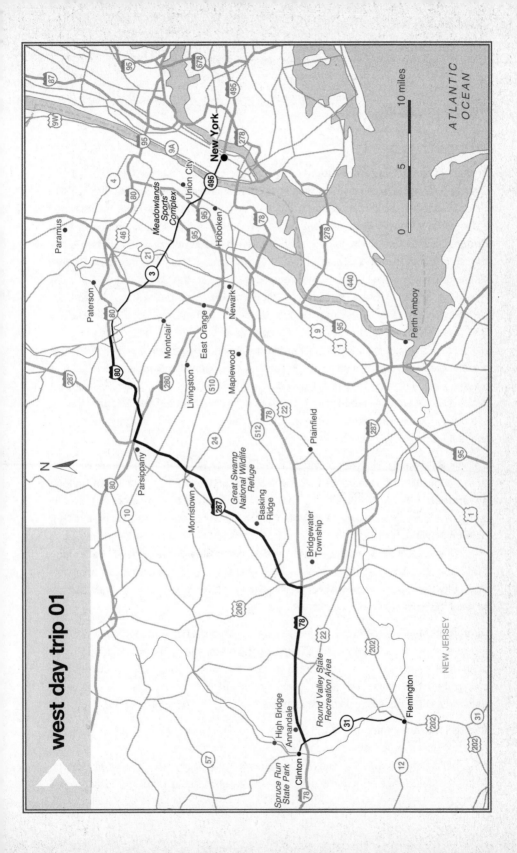

Merge onto NJ 23N toward I-80 W. Connect to I-287 S in Parsippany, then take I-78 W. Turn right on West Main Street.

where to go

Bridges of North Hunterdon County. Eight historic bridges exist near Clinton and it only takes about 2 hours to see them all. Start at the **Clinton Main Street Bridge.** Built in 1870, it's a two-span iron and truss bridge and one of only three that remain built by renowned builder William Corwin. Head to the nearby town of High Bridge for the **Arches of High Bridge.** Constructed over a six-year span in the mid-1800s, this quarter-mile bridge has two stone arches that open a path for the river and the road. Next up is the **Tisco Bridge.** It's the only historic steel bridge in the area and was built by the Carnegie Steel Company in 1910. At Voorhees State Park lies the **CCC Armco Bridge.** Built by the Civilian Conservation Corps in the 1930s and '40s, it utilizes stone from nearby foothills. The **Bartley Bridge** is a Pratt truss bridge built in 1887 that is now a steel stringer bridge due to it being widened by steel stringers in 1985. The **Wydner Farm Bridge** was built in 1860 and is one of more than 120 stone bridges in the county. **Changewater Bridge,** built in 1856, is an example of a high bridge. The bridge was razed in 1959 after the Western Railroad was discontinued. A stone arch bridge from 1900 lies beneath it. **Shoddy Mill Bridge** is the last of the magnificent eight. Built in 1868, this single-span truss bridge has eight panels and is one of the oldest surviving examples of such.

Hot Air Ballooning. Hunterdon County is a mecca for hot air balloon enthusiasts, and several companies operate hot air balloons in and around the Clinton area. **Avian Balloon Adventures** (908-713-6123) is one of the oldest and best-known operations in town (the company is based in Spokane, Washington) and has state-of-the-art equipment. **In Flight Balloon Adventures** (908-479-4674) has been providing rides since 1987 and specializes in engagement flights, dinner flights, and tethered rides. **New Jersey Hot Air Ballooning** (908-208-1869) flies year-round, seven days a week (weather permitting), at affordable rates. **Sky Sweeper Balloon Adventures** (800-462-3201) is a small local outfit but has some of the most affordable rates for couples' flights.

Hunterdon Museum of Art. 7 Lower Center St., Clinton; (908) 735-8415. One wouldn't expect such a pastoral town to have a noteworthy art museum. The Hunterdon Museum of Art dispels any notion that a country town can't be cultured. The small museum houses changing exhibits featuring established and emerging contemporary artists. The museum also hosts studio classes, workshops, summer camps for children, and lectures.

Red Mill Museum Village. 56 Main St., Clinton; (908) 735-4101. This 10-acre site boasts a 19th-century mill, schoolhouse, log cabin, quarry, screen house, and working blacksmith shop, among other structures. The M.C. Mulligan & Sons Quarry is the only one of its kind on the National Register of Historic Places. The main museum building houses 40,000 historic pieces in its permanent collection and hosts changing exhibits throughout the year. Visitors can rent canoes and take a paddle on the Raritan River. The museum hosts a Haunted Mill every Oct as well as paranormal events, wine tastings, Civil War reenactments, and a bluegrass festival.

where to shop

Bill Healy Designs. 14 Main St., Clinton; (908) 894-5400. Waterford Crystal master Bill Healy creates handmade crystal stemware, gifts, and art glass at this small shop. He also repairs and engraves crystal and glass by appointment. The shop also sells a small number of made-in-Ireland products.

Heartstrings. 10 Main St., Clinton; (908) 735-4020. This 2-room romantic shop features holiday, clothing, jewelry, antiques, custom bedding, and home decor items. Many of the ornaments have a vintage feel. Owner Carol Beder stocks items for the season so check back regularly.

Kindred Quilts. 21 East Main St., Clinton; (908) 730-8896. Kindred Quilts has all your quilting needs, from fabric to embroidery tools to needles and thread. The shop also instructs novice quilters.

Tante Kringle Christmas Cottage. 23 Old Rte. 22, Clinton. If you're serious about Christmas this is the store for you. Tante Kringle sells Christmas ornaments and tchotchkes year-round. Some of the European blown glass ornaments are especially beautiful and unique.

where to eat

Clinton House. 2 West Main St., Clinton; (908) 730-9300. Housed in a restored Victorian mansion, Clinton House serves homey continental fare in a lovely setting. Guests are treated like family and the service is very attentive. Choose from a wide array of items including traditional fare such as shrimp cocktail and not-so-traditional items such as snap turtle soup. The steaks are all grilled to perfection. If you're in a hurry, stop into the bakery for delicious cream puffs, éclairs, and French baguettes. $$.

Organic Leaf Cafe. 21 Main St., Clinton; (908) 713-1900. A small organic restaurant that offers a selection of fresh fruit smoothies, salads, sandwiches, fresh squeezed juices, and side dishes. Everything is 100 percent natural and certified organic. $.

Towne Restaurant. 31 Main St., Clinton; (908) 735-9250. For more than 30 years, the Rentoulis family has been serving fresh and hearty diner food to locals and tourists alike. The menu is your typical Greek diner menu with the requisite egg dishes and sandwiches. Come here for a quick breakfast or lunch. $$.

where to stay

Riverside Victorian Bed-and-Breakfast. 66 Leigh St., Clinton; (908) 238-0400. One of only two accommodations in town, the Riverside Victorian is exactly what it says. A large Victorian manse on the Delaware River. Built in 1882, the home features period antiques, family heirlooms, and reproduction pieces. The inn boasts 6 rooms, all outfitted with comfy quilts and antique beds (sleigh and wrought iron). The innkeeper makes her own Irish soda bread so make sure you have room for some. $$.

flemington

Drive south through rolling hills, down country byways until you hit the county seat of Flemington. Two thirds of the town is on the National Register of Historic Places. Acquired by William Penn in 1712, Flemington was soon settled by industrious English immigrants looking to farm the fertile land. After the Civil War, Germans repatriated here and began working in the various grist mills, copper mines, glass factories, pottery works, and iron foundries. The town gained worldwide attention in 1935 as the site of the Lindberg-Hauptmann trial (Bruno Richard Hauptmann was tried and convicted of kidnapping and murdering aviator Charles Lindberg's young son), which is recreated for the public every Oct.

getting there

It's about a 10-minute, 11-mile drive from Clinton to Flemington (barring traffic). Head south on NJ 31. Take a right on Walter E. Foran Boulevard, then turn right on North Main Street/CR 617.

where to go

Black River Railroad Historical Trust. 105 John Ringo Rd., Ringoes. Want to ride an old passenger train? Want to take your kids to meet Santa at the North Pole? Black River Railroad Historical Trust operates passenger trains throughout the year from Flemington Pennsylvania Station on Stangl Road and nearby Ringoes, New Jersey. Visitors can opt for various 75-minute journeys promoting local tourism and small-town railroading as well as special events such as murder mystery excursions, military history lectures, Santa visits, and corn maze sojourns. Guests ride aboard either steam locomotives or eco-friendly diesel-electric locomotives.

Northlandz. 495 US 202, Flemington; (908) 782-4022. Home to the world's largest model railroad, Northlandz is the brainchild of Bruce Williams Zaccagnino, who began building a model train set, complete with elaborate villages, 40-foot bridges, and thousands of lichen trees, as a way to while away the time while his house was being built. After 25 years of careful construction, the museum opened to the public. The 16-acre facility also houses a doll museum, La Peep dollhouse, art galleries, and a replica of a Victorian narrow gauge steam train.

where to shop

Liberty Village Premium Outlets. 1 Church St., Flemington; (908) 782-8550. Flemington has become a discount shopping mecca thanks to this outlet mall housed in a historic building downtown. Forty stores occupy the premises including Calvin Klein, Michael Kors, Carter's, Timberland, and Le Creuset.

where to eat

Il Mulino. 32 Fulper Rd., Flemington; (908) 806-0595. Let's face it. We can get great Italian food in the city but if you're on the road and still craving al dente pasta and savory sauces, Il Mulino can't be beat. This fine dining establishment serves Northern Italian cuisine, which can be heavy on the butter. Il Mulino uses fresh ingredients to amazing effect. $$$.

Theresa's Gourmet Deli and Cafe. 117 Broad St., Flemington; (908) 788-8886. Owner Theresa Faghani runs this homey cafe that is known for its buttery scones, steel cut oatmeal, burgers, chili, and salads. The baked goods are particular local favorites especially the homemade pies and cheesecakes. (Faghani never uses canned goods. Everything is made from scratch.) The staff is friendly and the prices are reasonable for the area. $$.

Vienna Bake Shop and Restaurant. 26 Main St., Flemington; (908) 782-2677. If you're still in the market for baked goods or want some strong coffee, head to this European-style bakery that packs a tasty wallop. Viennese tortes take center stage as do other sweet treats. Owners Fred and Erika Kuther welcome you with a smile. $$.

where to stay

Main Street Manor. 194 Main St., Flemington; (908) 782-4928. One of the nicer bed-and-breakfasts in Hunterdon County, Main Street Manor prides itself on offering unique accommodations. The 5 guest rooms are well appointed, with restored antiques, cozy homemade quilts, fresh flowers, and hypoallergenic down comforters. Owners Donna and Ken Arnold use locally sourced ingredients for breakfast and afternoon tea and even offer vegetarian and vegan specialties with advanced notice. $$.

Silver Maple Organic Farm and Bed-and-Breakfast. 483 Sergeantsville Rd., Flemington; (908) 237-2192. This stone farmhouse serves as the base for Silver Maple Organic Farm as well as its bed-and-breakfast lodgings. Situated in the Flemington countryside, Silver Maple has 5 suites and rooms, each with a different destination theme. The Sandbrook Room is the smallest with 2 twin beds and a cozy bathroom. The Santa Fe Suite is the largest and most luxurious with a king-size wrought iron bed as well as a smaller antique bed. All rooms are fashioned according to the style of the destination featured, with period furnishings and colorful bedding. Since Silver Maple serves as a farm as well as a bed-and-breakfast, owner Steven Noll is able to provide free range Amish meats and eggs as well as vegan and vegetarian options. The estate also features a pool, hot tub, and tennis court. The grounds are lovely, with plentiful flowers and sheep. $$.

day trip 02

west

>>>

the holy land:
bethlehem, pennsylvania
nazareth, pennsylvania

"Oh come all ye faithful . . . " And they do in droves, especially during the holiday season. The twin cities of Bethlehem and Nazareth, Pennsylvania, aren't anywhere near as holy as their namesakes in the Middle East but they still take Christmas seriously. So seriously in fact that you'll be hard-pressed not to get into the holiday spirit if you drive into town in December. The four-week Christkindlmarkt in Bethlehem and the Christmas Lovefeast in Nazareth have made the towns epicenters for the holidays, and these family friendly events offer a more authentic yuletide celebration than what you'd get at Rockefeller Center or Radio City Music Hall.

bethlehem

Nestled between Allentown and Easton, Bethlehem, aka Christmas City, has emerged as a year-round destination. The town was established on Christmas Eve 1741 by Moravians from Germany. The Moravians believed in communal living based on age and many of these historic buildings still stand downtown. The town was long a manufacturing center but has seen a rebirth as a trendy shopping and restaurant destination. "Restaurant Row" lures tourists as much as the multitude of 18th-century buildings, Star of Bethlehem, and Christmas festivities.

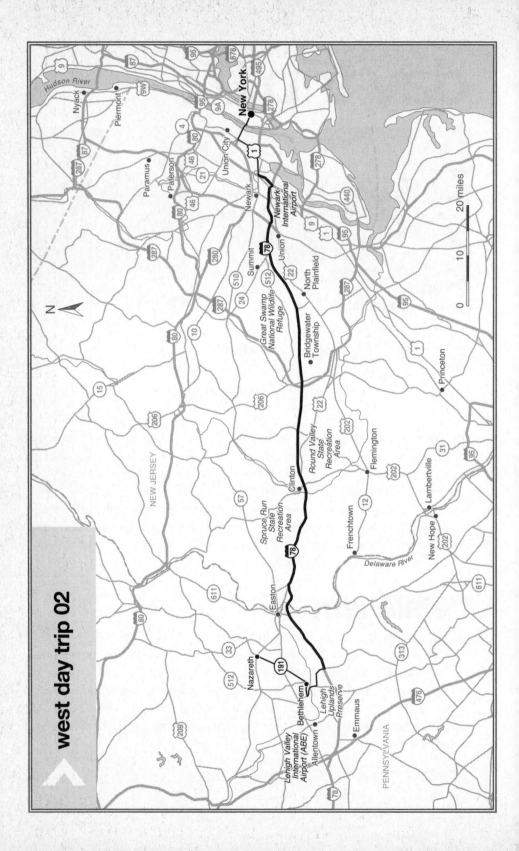

west day trip 02

getting there

Head down US 1 South to I-78 West. Take exit 67 to PA 412. Stay on PA 412 until you reach Stefko Boulevard. Take a right and follow the signs to the center of town. It's about an hour and a half drive.

where to go

Banana Factory. 25 West Third St., Bethlehem; (610) 332-1300. This 63,000-square-foot art space is home to 28 resident artists, three galleries, a glassblowing studio, and the Fowler Arts and Education Center. The on-site gift shop sells handmade crafts. The center wants to make art available to everyone and hosts a number of workshops and classes for children and adults alike.

Burnside Plantation. 1461 Schoenersville Rd., Bethlehem; (610) 868-5044. Many Moravians worked on farms in the Lehigh Valley and this large property was once owned by James Burnside. The homestead boasts a large farmhouse, garden, several barns, and outbuildings. Guided tours are available for large groups but self-guided tours are free of charge.

Kemerer Museum of Decorative Arts. 427 North New St., Bethlehem; (610) 868-6868. This 2-story brick building houses historic paintings, furniture, and crafts that showcase the region's German roots. The Bohemian glass exhibit tends to draw the most crowds. The museum also boasts the E. J. Prime dollhouse and toy collection, considered one of the best in the country.

Moravian Museum of Bethlehem. 66 West Church St., Bethlehem; (610) 867-0173. An expansive complex dedicated to the earliest European settlers of Bethlehem, who were known for their communal living spaces and progressive schooling. The three buildings that make up the complex are some of the oldest in the Lehigh Valley. **Gemeinhaus,** built in 1741, is the oldest building in the city and served several functions in the community including a school, church, and workspace. The Single Sister's House, 1744, showcases Germanic architecture and served as the home to the single female settlers who came to Bethlehem. **The Nain-Shober House** is an important structure as it symbolizes the good relationship between the Moravians and the Native Americans. **The Bethlehem Apothecary** housed the towns medicines and at one time was the oldest apothecary in operation in the United States.

where to shop

Clothesline Organics. 101 East Third St., Bethlehem; (610) 691-0111. Vegan and organic clothing lovers will enjoy the selection at this high-end boutique. Clothesline carries a wide array of eco-friendly, sweatshop-free designers including Steward+Brown, Edun, and Twice Shy and it's not just female centric. The store carries clothing for men and children as well.

Home & Planet. 26 East Third St., Bethlehem; (610) 866-7370. Head to this home goods store for furniture, house wares, and other items made of recycled and natural materials. Home & Planet carries products created by local and national artisans who are committed to helping the environment and reducing waste.

Moravian Book Shop. 428 Main St., Bethlehem; (610) 866-5481. Founded in 1745, this is the oldest continuously operating bookstore in the world. The Moravian Church, founded in Europe in 1457, helped establish it. The shop specializes in popular fiction, nonfiction tomes, and books about Lehigh Valley. The store also sells gifts, snacks, and accessories. The most popular selections revolved around ornaments with a Bethlehem theme.

Stone Soup Studios. 20 West Broad St., Bethlehem; (610) 867-4626. Stone Soup Studios boasts a selection of unique and limited-edition items made in the USA. From handmade jewelry to handpainted scarves to baby bibs to one-of-a-kind decorative pieces, customers come back regularly to see what's new.

where to eat

Apollo Grill. 85 West Broadway, Bethlehem; (610) 865-9600. One of the top restaurants in town, Apollo Grill serves a variety of Green and Mediterranean specialties in a fun setting. The salad selection is very extensive as is the pizza and sandwich selections. Locals like to head here for romantic dinners that involve great cocktails and dishes such as jerk pork tenderloin, Australian lamb shank, and grilled meats and fish. $$.

Bethlehem Brewworks. 569 Main St., Bethlehem; (610) 882-1300. Established in Bethlehem long before the town's rebirth, this gastro pub specializes in local microbrews as well as single malt scotch, bourbon, and martinis. The pub's Steelgaarden Lounge has more than 100 Belgian brews available. Much of the food menu are brewpub staples but the eatery also serves a number of Pennsylvania Dutch specialties such as bratwurts, pierogies, and pork schnitzel. $$.

Bolete Restaurant and Inn. 1740 Seidersville Rd., Bethlehem; (610) 868-6505. Bolete, meaning wild mushroom in Latin, is a back-to-basics locavore haven. The restaurant has garnered praise by local publications as well as *Condé Nast Traveler*. And with good reason. The innovative American fare is prepared in-house: breads, pastas, stocks, and sauces are all made on the premises (the restaurant smokes its own fish and meat as well). Vegetarians are welcome as are gluten-free and anyone else with a food allergy. The menu changes seasonally, sometimes even weekly. $$$.

where to stay

Sands Casino and Resort. 77 Sands Blvd., Bethlehem; (877) 726-3777. The newest addition to downtown Bethlehem, the Sands Casino and Resort now has high-end lodging to compliment its table games and Emeril restaurants. The 300-room hotel, an offshoot of the Las Vegas casino hotel, has 17 suites, five hospitality suites, an indoor pool, and a small fitness center. $$$.

Sayre Mansion Inn. 250 Wyandotte St., Bethlehem; (610) 882-2100. The Sayre Mansion Inn is one of Lehigh Valley's premier bed-and-breakfasts. The bed-and-breakfast serves as both a relaxing hotel and as a business center. Leisure guests can select from 19 guest rooms in the main house or three carriage house suites. Each room is uniquely furnished with a mix of restored antiques and modern furniture. Most rooms have a neutral color scheme but with pops of muted red, green, or blue. The conservatory room, with its plentiful skylights, is probably the most special. The carriage house has three lavish, large suites that feel like home. Business travelers will cheer for the hotel's corporate rates, meeting space, and amenities. $$$.

nazareth

Driving to Nazareth, you'll see the incongruous site of farmland abutting suburban sprawl. The town is worlds away from what it must have been like in the 1700s, when Moravian immigrants first settled the land. Still, one can admire the open pastures and the odd old homestead as well as the site of several wineries dotting the landscape as if they took the wrong turn at Napa. Life here is still slow-paced even though the town was a cement manufacturing mecca for much of the 20th century, attracting plentiful workers. Most of the workers are gone but the factories and their historical significance remain. The town gets dolled up at Christmas when tourists flock to the area to make their annual "pilgrimage."

getting there

The town is just a simple 9-mile, 20-minute drive from Bethlehem. Take PA 191 north towards Nazareth Bethlehem Pike. Turn left at South Broad Street.

where to go

C. F. Martin Guitar Company Museum. 510 Sycamore St., Nazareth; (610) 759-2837. Forget Gibson. Forget Fender. The oldest and most renowned guitar maker is C. F. Martin. Established in 1833, the C. F. Martin Guitar Company is American's largest and the world's oldest maker of fine acoustic guitars. The museum displays more than 170 handmade guitars and allows guests to indulge their inner rock star by playing limited-edition and high-end models.

Gray Cottage. 26 South Whitfield St., Nazareth; (610) 759-5070. Built in 1740, this log cabin is the oldest Moravian building in the country. It once housed the Moravian school for boys and the widows of Nazareth and Bethlehem.

Moravian Historical Society and Whitefield House Museum. 214 East Center St., Nazareth; (610) 759-5070. If you're interested in Moravian culture and their influence on the social and religious fabric of America, head to this museum. The Moravian Church is not as big as it once was but the Historical Society, established in 1857, kept genealogical records as well as decorative arts and artifacts from the church's past.

where to stay

Classic Victorian Estate Inn. 35 North New St., Nazareth; (610) 759-8276. The Classic Victorian Estate Inn is a welcoming colonial building in historic Nazareth. Geraniums greet you as you walk on the porch. The 3 rooms are each designed with vintage furniture and white bedding. Two have four posters, one a high back. All have en suite bathrooms and tons of old-fashioned charm. Owners Irene and Dan Sokolowski are extremely friendly and love helping guests plan their stay. $$.

worth more time

Nearby **Easton** isn't known for its Christmas celebrations but is worth a side trip, if time allows. The city has historical significance as the site of one of the three original readings of the Declaration of Independence. It's also home to The Crayola Factory and the National Canal Museum, both offering fun-filled activities for the entire family. The city isn't without its holiday traditions, however. The Peace Candle is illuminated every December in Centre Square's soldiers' monument as a homage to fallen soldiers from the Civil War.

day trip 03

west

>>> **ethnic tapestries:**
hoboken, new jersey
union city, new jersey

Sometimes day trips don't involve much driving or train travel and these are the types of trips to take if you want to get out of the city and back in no time at all. On the outskirts of New York City lie two cities that have a lot of history and culture and getting there is a piece of cake. Hoboken is best known as the birthplace of Frank Sinatra and baseball. It's also home to a thriving dining scene, one of New Jersey's best, and a mecca for singles and bicyclists. Union City is one of the most densely populated cities in the United States and has been home to a microcosm of the world: from the Dutch to the English to Germans, Armenians, Greeks, Latin Americans, and, most uniquely, Cubans. This influx resulted in a unique cultural and culinary history that remains today.

hoboken

Frank Sinatra, baseball, and Elia Kazan's *On the Waterfront*. From the time the city was founded by Henry Hudson in 1609, Hoboken has been a thriving community of immigrants, artists, and innovators. Today, the square-mile city is almost considered the sixth borough of New York City due to its proximity to Manhattan. The town boasts a multitude of historic buildings and sites, streets named after former U.S. presidents, and a pretty waterfront with high-rise condos and a W hotel from which to admire the flickering lights of downtown Manhattan across the water.

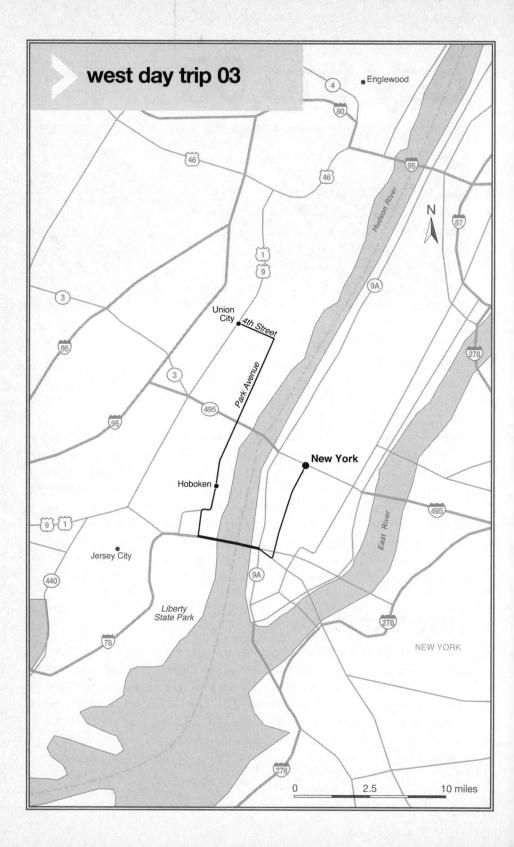

getting there

Take a Path train from downtown or Midtown Manhattan to Hoboken Terminal. Path train stops are 33rd, 23rd, 14th, Ninth, and Christopher Streets in Manhattan on the west side. Some Path stations can be transferred to via subway connections. It's an extra fare so don't use your Metrocard. The trip takes about 17 minutes from the 33rd Street Path Station (midtown), 11 minutes from Christopher Street (downtown).

If you're determined (and brave enough) to drive there, it can take a bit longer than the train. Take the Holland Tunnel to I-78. Take a right on Marin Boulevard. Take a right on Observer Highway and a left on Park Avenue. It takes about 20 minutes, without traffic.

where to go

Castle Point. Castle Point on Hudson, Hoboken. Built in 1854 by Edwin Augustus Stevens, son of Hoboken first-son Colonel John Stevens (the elder Stevens bought the entire town after the Revolutionary War), the serpentine rock "castle" once overlooked all of New York City (it's the highest point in all of Hoboken). Today, the 55-acre site is the home of the Stevens Institute of Technology, the oldest school of its kind in the country. Only the original Gate House remains as the home was demolished in 1959.

Frank Sinatra Walking Tour. So many buildings in the town of Hoboken lay claim to Frank Sinatra that to list them all would make for a separate tome altogether. Visitors should hit the Hoboken Historical Museum for a walking map of the numerous sites dedicated to Ol' Blue Eyes. Their suggested itinerary takes 2 hours and hits his birthplace as well as places

hoboken's favorite son

Long before Francis Albert Sinatra became Ol' Blue Eyes, he was the son of poor Italian immigrants living in Hoboken, New Jersey. The Hoboken of Sinatra's childhood was much different than the trendy "sixth New York City borough" it is today. The Italian enclave was home to thousands of immigrants, working on the dock or in area factories for a mere pittance. Sinatra's mother had high hopes for her crooner son. Realizing his immense talent, she pushed the younger Sinatra to sing in public. His first major performance was in a singing troupe called the Hoboken Four on the radio show Major Bowes and His Original Amateur Hour. *Fame soon came calling, and Sinatra went solo eventually heading to Hollywood where he would become a bonafide movie star and where he married starlets Ava Gardner and Mia Farrow. Frank Sinatra died of a heart attack in 1998 and the town enthusiastically celebrates his birth every Dec.*

at which he performed. The tour starts at **415 Monroe St.,** which is the house in which Francis Albert Sinatra was born in 1915. **333 Jefferson St.** was once the site of Marty O'Brien's Bar, where Sinatra first sang as a child. **610 Adams St.** was where Sinatra and a group of friends would sing acapella. **Leo's Grandezvous at 200 Grand St.** was a favorite watering hole of Sinatra's, and the owners still have the chair on which he sat. **909 Hudson St.** housed the home Sinatra bought his parents once he became famous. **Frank Sinatra Memorial Park** was dedicated to the singer in 1998. It has amazing views of the New York City skyline.

Hoboken Historical Museum & Cultural Center. 1301 Hudson St., Hoboken; (201) 656-2240. Housed in the former Bethlehem Steel Shipyard building, the Hoboken Historical Museum educates the public about the city's rich history and culture. Much of the artwork depicts local scenes or was painted by a local artist. The museum has a revolving set of special exhibits, events, and lectures and offers educational programs for all ages.

Mile Square Theatre. 720 Monroe St., Hoboken; (201) 683-7014. Located in the new Monroe Center, this small theater troupe promotes the stage arts in Hudson County. Mile Square Theatre produces new and classic works as well as teaches classes and conducts community-based projects and lectures. The troupe has performed *A Midsummer Night's Dream* and the *Scams of Scapin* among other historic works.

Stephen Collins Foster House. 601 Bloomfield St., Hoboken. The composer of diddies "Oh! Susanna" and "Camptown Races" lived in this orange brick row house in 1854, and it is said the city was the inspiration of "Jeanie with the Light Brown Hair."

Sybil's Cave. Castle Point on Hudson, Hoboken. Buried below the Stevens Institute of Technology is Sybil's Cave, site of the grisly murder of Mary Rogers in 1841 (Edgar Allan Poe based his story, "The Mystery of Marie Roget" on this case). The cave was opened in 1832, drew crowds by the hundreds in the 19th century, and inspired countless legends and myths. The city health department closed it down in the 1880s due to environmental concerns. It reopened in 2008 and is 17 feet in length.

where to shop

Washington Street plays host to the heart of Hoboken's shopping scene. You can spend a couple of hours strolling in and out of the stores, but here are some highlights.

Aaraa. 628 Washington St., Hoboken; (201) 386-0101. An Asian-inspired boutique that sells clothing, decorative items, jewelry, accessories, and handbags. Many of the items were imported from India, and the store hosts numerous sales throughout the year that offer deep discounts on much of the merchandise.

Air Studios Boutique. 55 First St., Hoboken; (201) 239-1511. Air Studios has a feel of a New York City boutique and small wonder when much of the selection is pricey designer apparel from the likes of Kenzo, Catherine Malandrino, and Philip Lim. The selection is varied and stylish but is not for the budget minded. Most items run in the $300 to $500 range. But you'll wear the heck out of whatever you buy.

Tunes. 225 Washington St., Hoboken; (201) 653-3355. A throwback to old-style music stores, Tunes is a cozy, unpretentious record store that stocks a wealth of vinyl and CDs, much of it imports or rare and/or gently used. You can unearth some gems in the bargain bin. The staff is friendly and helpful and sells tickets to shows at nearby Maxwell's.

where to eat

Carlo's Bake Shop. 95 Washington St., Hoboken; (201) 659-3671. Since 1910, this bakeshop has been winning accolades in Hoboken but it wasn't until the Food Network chose the bakery for its *Cake Boss* show that business really boomed. Owner Buddy Valastro makes intricate cakes and pastries, many from recipes passed down through the generations. Expect a line as the shop is teeming with people. $$.

Maxwell's Restaurant & Bar. 1039 Washington St., Hoboken; (201) 653-1703. While most patrons head to this iconic club for great rock shows (many a famous band got their American debut here), the bar serves food into the late hours so a nosh shouldn't be overlooked because you're swilling a delicious craft brew. The nachos are enormous and can easily fill up two people. Still, it's the inexpensive drinks and music that are the real lure. $$.

"the best club in new york— even though it's in new jersey"

Thank The New Yorker *for that headline. In the early 1990s, the literary icon dubbed* **Maxwell's** *(1039 Washington St.; www.maxwellsnj.com) in Hoboken the best music club in the New York City area. I would have to wholeheartedly agree. Not just for the intimate ambience but also for the caliber of performers who've played there.*

For many a struggling band, getting a gig at Maxwell's is tantamount to making it big. Many a famous band cemented its reputation by playing in the small venue (capacity is just 200). Eighties icon New Order played one of its first American concerts there. In 1989, Nirvana appeared there in support of its debut album Bleach, *still considered one of Kurt Cobain and co.'s most raw performances outside of Seattle. Oasis appeared there in 1994, one of its first U.S. shows, ushering in the Britpop revolution of the 1990s. Even Bruce Springsteen paid a visit, filming his "Glory Days" video at Maxwell's in 1985.*

Zafra Kitchen. 301 Willow Ave., Hoboken; (201) 610-9801. If you're in the mood for good Latin/Cuban fare, Zafra Kitchen won't disappoint. This BYO restaurant serves small plates and entrees using traditional recipes and ingredients. The Quesadilla de Hongos is great for vegetarians. The ham croquettes are a Cuban staple and Zafra's version made my companion's mouth water. If you bring your own wine, the restaurant will turn it into Sangria, for an extra charge. $$.

where to stay

W Hoboken. 225 River St., Hoboken; (201) 253-2400. The latest W to hit the New York City environs, the W Hoboken has some of the best views of Manhattan of any hotel in the tri-state area. The hotel boasts 225 chic rooms with the much ballyhooed W bed and modern amenities such as Whatever/Whenever service, a media library, goose down duvets, and Bliss Spa bath products. The hotel boasts several dining options as well as a trendy bar. $$$.

union city

A microcosm of American ethnic groups, Union City is an urban metropolis teeming with people who can trace their lineage to settlers from various parts of Europe, Africa, and Latin America. The most visible of these groups are the Cubans, who first settled in town after the infamous Mariel boatlift in 1980. Nicknamed "Havana on the Hudson," Union City boats a unique Latin flavor that is visible in its cuisine, music, and cigar-making facilities.

getting there

Head back to the historic Hoboken Terminal and catch a New Jersey North Bergen Light Rail train from Hoboken to Tonelle Avenue/North Bergen. The train trip takes about 16 minutes. Walk 4 blocks east out of the station until you get to the center of Union City. Trains run regularly throughout the day.

By car, it's about a 5- to 10-minute drive to Union City. Go north on Park Avenue, take a left on 11th Street and a right on Willow Avenue. Merge onto Park Avenue. Continue on Park until you hit 45th Street. Take a left and you're in the center of town.

where to go

Park Performing Arts Center. 560 32nd St., Union City; (201) 865-6980. Noteworthy artists and performers, such as the Maria Benitez Spanish Dance Company and the late Johnny Cash, made this large center the brightest of its kind in the area. The focal point of the center is the 1,400-seat Park Theatre, built in 1931 by a German-Catholic congregation. The center produces a diverse range of programs from concerts to plays to dance performances. It also runs exhibits and education programs that center on New Jersey history and culture. The center runs *The Passion Play* every year in March.

where to shop

Boquilla Cigar Company. 2314 Summit Ave., Union City; (201) 867-8260. Cuban immigrant Jose Suarez and his stepson Bob Ramos run this small factory that makes handmade cigars in the Cuban style. The selection is varied but inexpensive. The factory sells a signature cigar brand that the workers meticulously roll in the back room.

where to eat

Beyti Kebab Restaurant. 4105 Park Ave., Union City; (201) 865-6281. Not every restaurant in Union City specializes in Cuban food. Beyti is known for authentic Turkish halal cuisine with great kebabs as well as vegetarian staples such as eggplant. The eggplant appetizers can fill you up quickly. Leave some room for the massive kebab platters or combination platters that sometimes include gyro, chicken, and lamb patties. The restaurant hosts a belly dancer and traditional Turkish musicians every Saturday night. $$.

El Artesano. 4101 Bergenline Ave., Union City; (201) 867-7341. A local legend, El Artesano serves Cuban stables such as Cuban sandwiches, pulled pork, beef stew, and rice and beans in a casual, family friendly setting. Lunchtime is the best time to head here as the crowds aren't as dense. Try the Cuban style hamburger. It's hearty and very filling. $$.

Mi Bandera. 518 32nd St., Union City; (201) 348-2828. One of the most authentic Cuban restaurants in town, it also serves some of the best Churrasco in the area. The menu is extensive and fairly priced with weekday lunch specials that offer heaping amounts of meat, plantains, rice, and beans. Plantain baskets are a good start to any meal as you have your choice of filling (the garlic shrimp is a local fave). $$.

northeast

>>>

day trip 01

northeast

fall foliage:
ridgefield, connecticut
kent, connecticut
litchfield, connecticut

Open air, meandering rivers, and rolling hills take you from suburban sprawl to the Litchfield Hills, a historic district in Northwestern Connecticut that is often at the top of "Best of" fall foliage lists. Canopies of trees cover two-lane roads that lead you from artsy Ridgefield to historic Litchfield and to bucolic Kent. All three towns offer solid dining and lodging options, with Ridgefield being the most developed of the three. Kent is the most tranquil, thanks to less development and an adherence to old-fashioned ways. Litchfield has a long tradition of being progressive and energetic. The trio of towns is a popular destination in the fall when the riotous seasonal leaf display occurs.

ridgefield

Northwestern Connecticut has long had a tradition of fostering the arts, and the town of Ridgefield is the epicenter for the arts in the area. Much like Manchester, Vermont, the town is replete with Victorian homes with wraparound porches and quaint mom-and-pop shops abutting more well-known brands. The town was once all about antiques but that's been superseded by home decor shops and art galleries.

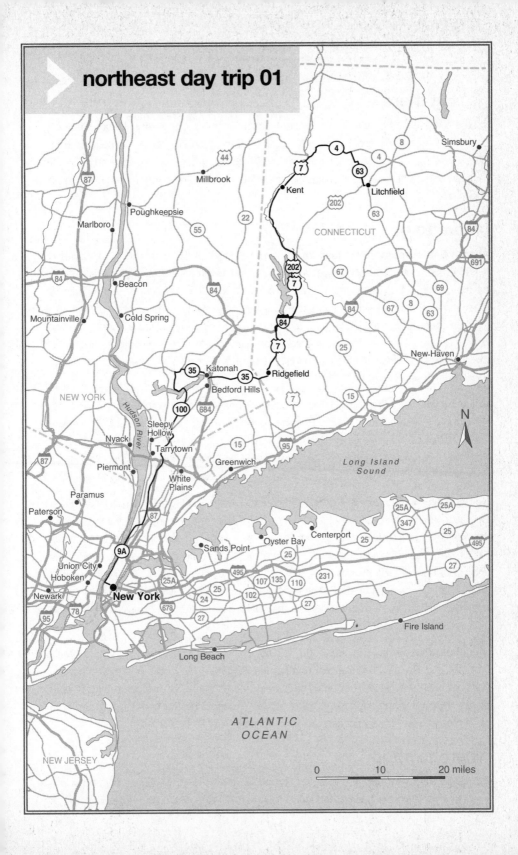

northeast day trip 01

getting there

Take the Westside Highway to the Henry Hudson Parkway. The Henry Hudson Parkway becomes the Saw Mill River Parkway N. Take exit 6 to Katonah. Stay on the right ramp for CT 35, and take a right onto CT 35. Stay on CT 35/Cross River Road. Take a left on CT 35/Main Street until you get to Ridgefield. It's about an hour and a half drive in good traffic conditions.

where to go

Aldrich Contemporary Art Museum. 258 Main St., Ridgefield; (203) 438-4519. Founded in 1964, this contemporary art museum is one of the few in the United States that doesn't have a permanent collection (it sold those works in 1981). The museum boasts exhibits by emerging and lesser-known artists as well as education programs and lectures for the entire family. Founder Larry Aldrich was an avid art collector who envisioned a space at which contemporary art was accessible to people of all walks of life. The museum is housed in the historic "Old Hundred" building on Main Street that served as a grocery store and post office for 100 years.

Ballard Park. Main Street, Ridgefield. Although it bears small resemblance to the original Revolutionary War–era park, 5-acre Ballard Park is still worth a visit for its perennial gardens and greenhouse. Former owner Elizabeth Ballard deeded the estate to the Ridgefield Garden Club which has managed to keep the estate in pristine condition—many of the trees and shrubs remain—while enhancing the walkways and bandstand.

Keeler Tavern Museum & Garden House. 132 Main St., Ridgefield; (203) 431-0815. Built as a private residence in 1713 but turned into a tavern and inn in 1772, the Keeler Tavern was fired upon by British troops during the Revolutionary War while proprietor, Thomas Keeler, was making musket balls in the basement. You can still see one of the cannonballs imbedded in a wall. The site has been on the National Register of Historic Places since 1982 and became a museum in 1966. The museum preserves the town's history by exhibiting documents and records from the families that resided in and ran the tavern throughout the 18th and 19th centuries.

Ridgefield Playhouse. 80 East Ridge St., Ridgefield; (203) 438-5795. From Marcel Marceau to Joan Baez to The Bacon Brothers, the Ridgefield Playhouse has played host to enthusiastic crowds as well as equally enthusiastic performers over the course of its 10-year history. Housed in the auditorium of the old high school, the Playhouse hosts concerts, plays, operatic performances, and movie screenings.

where to shop

Books on the Common. 404 Main St., Ridgefield; (203) 431-9100. Since 1984, book lovers from around Northwestern Connecticut have headed to Books on the Common for new, used, and rare books. The 2,100-square-foot space boasts shelves of critically acclaimed fiction as well as rare and unique nonfiction tomes. The store hosts book readings, signings, and storytime events for children.

Deborah Ann's Sweet Shop. 381 Main St., Ridgefield; (203) 438-0065. This old-fashioned chocolate shop opened in 1998. Homemade chocolates get top billing—the shop creates its confections at a 4,000-square-foot facility in nearby Brookfield—but other sweets aren't neglected. Choose from an array of licorice, hard candy, and other confections lovingly displayed in glass mason jars.

Nancy O. 1 Big Shop Lane, Ridgefield; (203) 431-2266. Housed in a former carriage house, this charming boutique is for the knitter in your life. The shop has a wealth of yarn and knitting supplies such as needles, patterns, and sig'nits. It also hosts instructional classes for individuals and groups. The shop offers a small selection of jewelry, gifts, and clothing.

Turkey Ridge. 1 Bailey Ave., Ridgefield; (203) 431-1255. From jewelry to home goods to decorative pillows to local artwork and antiques, Turkey Ridge offers a diverse range of products for the home and person. You're likely to come across a wealth of one-of-a-kind items at this spacious shop that is a local favorite.

where to eat

Bailey's Backyard. 23 Bailey Ave., Ridgefield; (203) 431-0796. Cozy and romantic, Bailey Backyard is the brainchild of two CIA grads who have made the American bistro one of Ridgefield's favorite eateries. The restaurant uses only zero trans fat oils to create healthy but hearty fare. Popular dishes include coffee braised short ribs and seared duck breast with cranberry ginger chutney. The wine list is small but offers a variety of crowd pleasing selections. $$$.

Cafe Luc's. 3 Big Shop Lane, Ridgefield; (203) 894-8522. Since 2001, Cafe Luc's has been creating Parisian cuisine in a charming setting (a terrace is open during the summer). After opening a restaurant in Greenwich Village (the now defunct Les Deux Gamins) and another cafe in Chelsea, owner Hervé Aussavis moved to Ridgefield with his family to open Cafe Luc. He also has Le Gamin in Soho, which he opened in 1992. Cafe Luc offers classic dishes such as Niçoise salad, snails in Pernod, and cassoulet. $$.

Ross' Bread. 109 Danbury Rd., Ridgefield; (203) 438-4822. Ross Schneiderman has been crafting delicious breads and pastries for many years. Trained in Tuscany, Schneiderman specializes in classic American and European delicacies such as croissants, cookies, scones, monkey bread, and Tuscan olive oil cake. Most of the ingredients are organic or locally sourced and everything is baked on the premises daily. $.

where to stay

Elms Inn. 500 Main St., Ridgefield; (203) 438-2541. Nestled on 3 verdant acres, the 18th-century Elms Inn offers 19 rooms and suites styled with period furnishings and private baths as well as modern amenities such as high-speed Wi-Fi, air conditioning, and cable TV. Guests receive their breakfast in-room each morning and are free to stroll the lovely gardens. $$.

Stonehenge Inn and Restaurant. 35 Stonehenge Rd., Ridgefield; (203) 438-6511. This historic estate delights visitors to Ridgefield. The 16 rooms in 3 buildings evoke a time gone by. Antiques and four-poster beds dominate the cozy environs. While the standard rooms offer anything you could want from a bed-and-breakfast lodging, it's the guest cottage that deserves most of the praise. The design is clean and fresh, even though antiques abound. Locals have long praised the Stonehenge restaurant for its commitment to pampering guests with innovative takes on local favorites. The *New York Times* gave it an Excellent rating. $$.

kent

The village of Kent, established in 1739, is a popular destination for foliage lovers (it was named the top New England foliage destination in *Yankee* magazine), with myriad spots for your viewing pleasure. The town is situated near two state parks. Macedonia Brook State Park is where most leaf lovers head as it offers 2,300 acres of unobstructed trails up the Catskill and Taconic mountains. Kent Falls State Park encompasses part of the Appalachian trail and hikers can enjoy the vistas, whatever their experience level. It's also the site of Kent Falls, the largest waterfall in the state. The town is home to design shops and small galleries.

getting there

Take CT 35 N to US 7 N/US 202 E, past rock slides and some industrial parks until you see open fields. There is a cemetery on the left side of the street when you come into town. A covered bridge at Balls Bridge Road takes you over a canal with a powerful spillway to the right.

where to go

Connecticut Museum of Mining and Mineral Science. US 7, Kent. This new museum showcases the unique history of Northwestern Connecticut, which once had a store of valuable mineral deposits and boasted 600 mines when at its peak. The museum is located on what was once an iron refinery and houses underground exhibits focusing on the local mining industry as well as a collection of minerals and ores from the area.

the gingerbread man

*In 2010, Kent, Connecticut, sponsored its first annual **Gingerbread Festival** (www .kentct.com). The family friendly monthlong event heralded the start of the holiday season, with food, music, and shopping all taking center stage. More than 50 village merchants in the charming hamlet displayed gingerbread creations in shop windows for passersby to enjoy and vote on. The winner received a $400 prize. The festival, which runs from late November to December 31, features Santa photo ops, concerts, tree lighting ceremonies, and readings by local authors.*

Kent Falls State Park. US 7, Kent Falls. The most scenic and beautiful part of Kent, it's just a short 5-minute drive up US 7 from main street. You can't miss the falls as you get into town; they are visible to the right of the road. The falls run 70 feet down the rock wall. Park your car and walk through the small covered bridge that leads you to a picnic area and paved steps to the falls. Guests with fishing licenses can fish for trout in the small stream by the bridge. If you're adventurous, hike the ¼-mile trail adjacent to the falls. Springtime is the best time to visit as the winter snowmelt makes for a more dramatic waterfall.

Sloane Stanley Museum. 31 US 7, Kent; (860) 927-3849. Painter and author Eric Sloane illustrated more than 30 books and collected American artifacts, tools, and gifts. This museum houses his collection of hand tools and Americana. His art studio showcases examples of his work and looks as if the artist just stepped away from his easel. The museum grounds also include the Kent Iron Furnace, which produced pig iron for 70 years.

where to shop

Kent Goods. 3 Old Barn Rd., Kent; (203) 770-3583. Kent Goods sells local produce as well as homemade oils, vinegars, jams, and kitchen items. The shop has a small selection of vintage goods and fair trade items. Many of the items are from local establishments such as Three Sisters Farm in Essex, Woodstock Hill Preserves in Woodstock, and a variety of unique sea salt from Maine.

Morrison Gallery. 8 Old Barn Rd., Kent; (860) 927-4501. Contemporary art and sculpture are the highlights of this 7,000-square-foot gallery that is anything but rustic. More than 32 international artists are represented including Sandra Filippuci, Hugh O'Donnell, and Hans Hofmann. The gallery hosts openings with live jazz throughout the year and exhibits by renowned artists.

Terston Home Accents and Womenswear. 31 North Main St., Kent; (860) 927-3226. Located in a historic Victorian home, Terston is a lifestyle store that boasts home goods, women's clothing, and fragrances. Many of the items are trendy—the fragrance selection alone has a number of high-end European brands—and colorful, echoing the design aesthetic of owner Geraldine Woodruff.

where to eat

Fife 'n Drum Restaurant. 53 North Main St., Kent; (860) 927-3509. The Revolutionary War–themed Fife 'n Drum opened its doors in 1973, when the town didn't allow women to sit at the bar. Women and men head here for the delicious duck flambé and filet mignon flambé as well as Dolph Trayman's delicate piano playing. The restaurant's wine list has garnered the Best of Award of Excellence by *Wine Spectator* magazine. $$.

Millstone Cafe and Bakery. 14 North Main St., Kent; (860) 592-0500. The menu at this new eatery is locally sourced, from the dairy and grains to the meat and produce. Owners John Cummins and Carol Hawran both trained at the Culinary Institute of America and wanted to serve farm-fresh food in a family friendly atmosphere. During the summer months, enjoy your lunch or dinner on the outdoor deck and porch. $$$.

Villager Restaurant. 28 North Main St., Kent; (860) 927-1555. The Villager restaurant is a Kent mainstay mainly for its hearty breakfasts but even more so for its traditional Mexican dishes. The restaurant is casual and reasonably priced and offers discounts to senior citizens. It also offers a revolving list of daily lunch specials. $$.

where to stay

Inn at Kent Falls. 107 Kent Cornwall Rd.; (860) 927-3197. Built in the early 1900s, the Inn at Kent Falls is nestled in a lovely open area, amid landscaped gardens. The Inn has six accommodations, three of which are suites. All rooms have period antiques, elegantly appointed furnishings, and private baths. Suites have private fireplaces and large bathrooms with claw-foot tubs. Many of the rooms have amazing views of Cobble Brook, which runs through much of the property. The grounds feature meandering gardens, footpaths, and an in-ground pool. $$$.

Starbuck Inn. 88 North Main St., Kent; (860) 927-1788. A love of people and an attention to small details make Starbuck Inn stand out from other bed-and-breakfasts. Innkeeper Peter Starbuck has made his 5-room home inviting and charming. You'll want to come back. All rooms have comfortable beds and cotton linens. The standard rooms have queen beds and en suite baths with showers. The king room has a bathtub and the king suite, a private entrance, and an expansive living and bathing area with Frette towels and bathrobes. Head there in the off-season when rates are drastically discounted. $$$.

litchfield

The rolling hills continue to Litchfield, the most historic of the three towns on this day trip. Litchfield has a plethora of historic homes and buildings, many of which proudly display their dates of formation on their exteriors. Several historic sites surround lovely Litchfield Green in the center of town, including the Litchfield History Museum and Tapping Reeve, the oldest law school in the nation. Head further down Main Street and you'll see old homes, some dating back to the late 1700s that have been restored to their former glory.

getting there

Take US 7 North towards Litchfield. Turn right on Kent Road. Take CT 4 East. Take a right on Old Middle Street/CT 63 down to Litchfield. It's about a 22-minute drive, without traffic.

where to go

Litchfield History Museum. 7 South St., Litchfield; (860) 567-4501. Housing seven galleries of furniture, art, costumes, and housewares that recall Litchfield's past, the history museum hosts visitors and students who are interested in the area's history. Some galleries examine early American life while others have changing exhibits and products from America and beyond.

Mt. Tom State Park. US 202, Litchfield. The view from the top of Mt. Tom State Park, one of the oldest parks in the state, takes your breath away. The stone lookout tower at the peak offers spectacular views of area mountains. Autumnal splendor at its finest. The park has myriad hiking trails, a small beach and swimming area, and grills for cooking. Canoes and kayaks are available for rental.

Tapping Reeve House & Law School. 7 South St., Litchfield; (860) 567-4501. The oldest law school in the nation, Tapping Reeve doesn't take students anymore. Instead, visitors learn what it was like to be a law student in the early 19th century. Guides take visitors through role-playing activities and interpretive exhibits.

Walking Tour of Historic Litchfield. A number of historic buildings flank the Litchfield Green from churches to an apothecary shop to the county courthouse. The Litchfield Historical Society has a brochure that lists all the historic sites in town. Start on North Street at the oldest historic building in town, **The Painter House.** Built around 1685 in West Haven, Connecticut, it was transferred to Litchfield in 1959. George Washington supposedly slept at **Sheldon's Tavern,** ca. 1760. **Dr. Smith's Apothecary Shop,** ca. 1781, is considered the oldest commercial structure in town. South Street has **Moses and Jane Seymour's federal-style house,** which was built in 1817. **Oliver Wolcott Sr.'s house** was built in 1753. Wolcott was a signer of the Declaration of Independence.

where to shop

Guy Wolff Pottery. 1249 Bantam Rd., Bantam; (860) 567-5577. Located just outside Litchfield on US 202, Guy Wolff makes pottery for the rich and famous, including Martha Stewart. Since 1971, Wolff has created handmade red and white clay pots for gardeners around the area. Some of the items for sale are one-of-a-kind pieces so snatch them up if you can.

Toll House Antiques. 38 Old Turnpike Rd., Litchfield; (860) 567-3130. If you like country antiques, you'll love Toll House Antiques. Housed in a barnlike building, the shop sells furniture, stoneware, dishes, kitchen supplies, clocks, and bedding. The interior of the store looks like someone's old country store, with antiques lovingly displayed on wooden crates and shelves.

where to eat

The Village Restaurant. 25 West St., Litchfield; (860) 567-8307. An award-winning restaurant on the village square, The Village serves American and Italian favorites in an unpretentious setting. Portions are generous and the prices are reasonable. The tap room is a favorite watering hole for area locals. Prix fixe menus are available on Mon and Tues. $$.

West Street Grill. 43 West St., Litchfield; (860) 567-3885. A little bit of New York in Northwestern Connecticut, West Street Grill has been using local and seasonal ingredients in its continental cuisine since 1989. The decor is understated but utilizes innovative touches such as the Quimperware plates. Much of the food has an Asian or French element to it. Standout dishes include the diver scallops and short ribs of beef. $$.

where to stay

Litchfield Inn. 432 Bantam Rd., Litchfield; (860) 567-4503. The plantation-style Litchfield Inn is one of the area's largest, with 32 rooms. Each room and deluxe room has a private bath, cable TV, and individual heating/cooling units. Rooms have four-poster beds, kitschy quilts, and vintage furniture. Some units are wheelchair accessible. $$.

Tollgate Hill Inn and Restaurant. 571 Torrington Rd., Litchfield; (860) 567-1233. Tollgate Hill Inn is listed as the Captain William Bull Tavern (built in 1745) in the National Register of Historic Places. Welcoming weary travelers for centuries, the Tollgate Hill Inn has three lodging choices: The first is the aforementioned Captain William Bull Tavern. The 6 rooms feature Hunt Country pine and period antiques. It's as if you've gone back in time to jolly old England as it is reminiscent of a posting house. The second is the Captain William Bull House which has rooms a bit more lavish and modern with outdoor patios, full baths, and Wi-Fi. Third, the schoolhouse offers the most distinctive accommodations, with cozy and enchanting rooms. The Tollgate Tavern features hearty American fare in a cozy colonial setting. $$$.

day trip 02

northeast

coastal connecticut:
greenwich, connecticut
new haven, connecticut

The Connecticut coast is a year-round playground. During the summer, residents relax on sailboats as they travel up and down the Long Island Sound to various points in Connecticut and New York. During the winter, the towns dress up for the holidays, hosting festivals and Christmas fairs in town squares. Here we highlight two cities on the shoreline: Greenwich, with its storied history as a tony enclave, high real estate values and exclusivity; and New Haven, a culturally strong city thanks in no small part to Yale University.

greenwich

There are tony enclaves and then there are tony enclaves. Greenwich may have them all beat. Voted one of the best places to live in the United States and home to uber-wealthy hedge fund managers, Greenwich has some of the highest property values in the country. The town is so exclusive that it restricted beach access to town residents. Thankfully, that rule was overturned and the general public can now enjoy the pristine white sand at Greenwich Point. The town has three islands off coast, each with its unique appeal. Two are bird sanctuaries, the other known for its beach. Greenwich has managed to maintain its storied charm and uniqueness. For more information visit the Greenwich Chamber of Commerce at www.greenwichchamber.com.

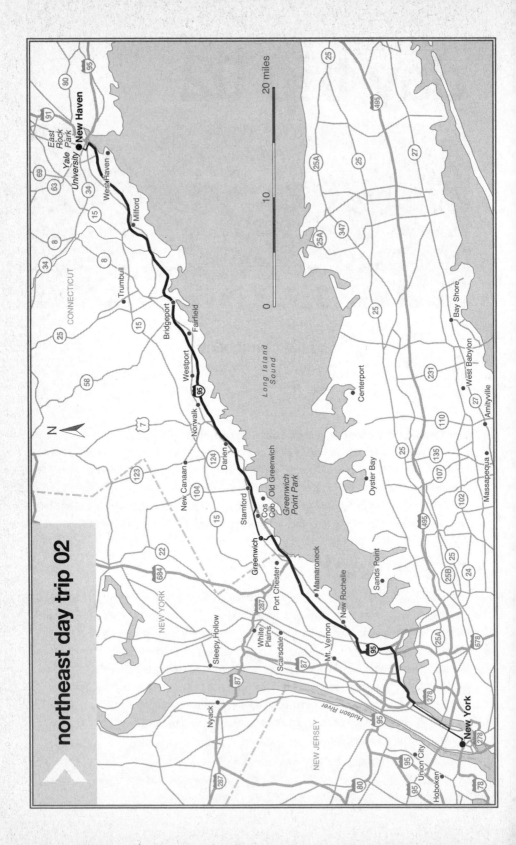

northeast day trip 02

getting there

From Grand Central Station, take a Metro-North New Haven line train from New York City to Greenwich. It's about a 50-minute trip from station to station. It's about a 57 minute drive from New York City. Take I-278 E/Bruckner Expressway toward New Haven. Connect to I-95 N/Bruckner Expressway. Take exit 3 for Arch Street in Greenwich.

where to shop

The heart of Greenwich's shopping is centered along **Greenwich Avenue,** (steps away from the train station) and **East Putnam Avenue.** Here high-end chains like Ralph Lauren, Saks Fifth Avenue, Lily Pulitzer, Kate Spade, Tiffany & Co., Baccarat, J. Crew, Lacoste, and Apple are sprinkled with independent stores—too many to list here, but suffice it to say, if you have money to spend you'll have no problem finding a place to spend it and if you are just window shopping there isn't a better place to do so. Here are just a couple of highlights located just off the beaten path:

Cook and Craft. 27 Arcadia Rd., Old Greenwich; (203) 637-2755. Housewares, stemware, dishes and other home goods get top billing at this high-end home store. Cook and Craft carry an array of organic and eco-friendly brands including Hillborn pottery, David Lory bowls and Ed Wohl cutting boards. Each item the store carries has been hand selected and tested by the owners. Located in Old Greenwich, but worth the short trip by car.

Splurge. 19A East Putnam Ave., Greenwich; (203) 869-7600. This small shop in a cute brick building stocks unique gifts for the entire family. Many of the items are one-of-a-kind and handmade. From handmade jewelry to home furnishings to decorative pieces to art-work, Splurge is a local favorite for its ever-changing selection of items.

where to go

The Bruce Museum. 1 Museum Dr., Greenwich; (203) 869-0376. Housed in a private home, The Bruce Museum is Greenwich's answer to New York City's Natural History Museum. The town-owned museum has a number of permanent and revolving exhibits that showcase science, art and natural phenomena. The permanent exhibit focuses on geology and ecology works. Docents lead museum tours, but visitors can opt to take self-guided audio tours instead.

Greenwich Point. Todd's Driftway and Shore Road, Greenwich. One of the nicest and most family friendly beaches in town. Greenwich Point is open from sunrise to sunset and offers fun for everyone in the family, whatever their outdoor interest. Besides the pristine beach, the park boasts jogging trails, areas to ride bicycles, fishing spots and picnic areas. The area is well known for shell fishing and great views of the ocean and surrounding land, which may be taken in from a number of conveniently-placed benches.

> ## ahoy captain!

*Greenwich, Connecticut, has always been a tony enclave. But if you head to the city and turn back to New York after a day of shopping and eating, you'd miss out on one of the town's best sites. Just 1 mile from the shore lies **Great Captain's Island** (www.greenwichct.org), named for Captain Daniel Patrick, the town's first military official (legend also has it that Captain Kidd buried gold and silver on the island but the treasure has never been found). The 17-acre island is a cherished bird sanctuary as well as a quiet recreation area with a beach, shelter, and restrooms. The site also boasts a small stone lighthouse, one of the northeast's best preserved. Visitors can head to the island by private boat or public ferry via the Arch Street Dock in Greenwich.*

Greenwich Symphony Orchestra. 10 Hillside Rd., Greenwich; (203) 869-2664. Established in 1958, the Greenwich Symphony Orchestra is one of the most storied orchestras not found in a big city. Performances are held at Greenwich High School's Hollister Auditorium. Summer concerts are held outdoors.

Putnam Cottage. 243 East Putnam Ave., Greenwich; (203) 869-9697. Built in the late 1600s, Putnam Cottage was once home to General Israel Putnam, a hero during the Revolutionary War. Students head here to learn about the area's role in the war and in American history.

where to eat

Many Greenwich restaurants offer great brunch deals—perfect to break up a day of shopping. Below are a few highlights. If you are looking for a lighter bite or something to go, you'll find plenty of options along The Avenue.

The Ginger Man. 64 Greenwich Ave.; (203) 861-6400; www.gingermangreenwich.com. New England Pub food—burgers, salads, fish, and beer are the centerpieces of this cozy tavern. The bar offers an impressive 23 beers on tap plus 60 bottled varieties. $$.

Greenwich Tavern. 1392 East Putnam Ave., Old Greenwich; (203) 698-9033; www.greenwichtavern.net. American fare. Come on the weekend for the Champagne brunch where you can grab some bubbly for half the price. Brunch standouts include a shrimp cobb salad, Maine lobster roll, eggs with short rib hash, and the "Earth & Ocean Benedict" (petit filet mignon and crabmeat served with a chipotle Hollandaise sauce). A prix fixe brunch menu is available for $19.95 and includes your choice of mimosa, bellini or bloody mary. $$.

My Favorite Place. 1 Strickland Rd., Greenwich; (203) 869-1500; www.myfavoriteplacect .net. This family friendly eatery caters to anyone looking for a quick nosh and is also welcoming to anyone with a food allergy. Many of the dishes are personally prepared by the owner. The fare is pretty standard—hot dogs, burgers, salads—but the portions are large and the owner is super friendly and accommodating. $$.

Restaurant Jean Louis. 61 Lewis St.; (203) 622-8450; www.restaurantjeanlouis.com. Known as one of the best French restaurants in the country, Restaurant Jean Louis certainly deserves those accolades. A James Beard Award winner, chef/owner Jean-Louis Gerin serves a 5-course degustation menu that is out of this world good. Guests can also enjoy a la carte selections. The artwork on the wall is for sale. $$$.

Thataway Cafe. 409 Greenwich Ave., Greenwich; (203) 622-0947; www.thatawaycafe .com. A casual and friendly dining spot, Thataway Cafe isn't a locavore eatery nor is it steeped in pretension. The restaurant serves American favorites such as burgers, nachos and salads. The prices are reasonable by Greenwich standards and the eatery is welcoming. Thataway showcases local and up and coming talent on Songwriters Den Thursday and urges patrons to perform during Karaoke Sundays. $$.

where to stay

Homestead Inn. 420 Field Point Rd., Greenwich; (203) 869-7500. With 18 rooms and suites, the Homestead Inn is one of Greenwich's finest lodging establishments. Each room is unique and has a queen or king bed, Frette linens and colorful decor, from the bedspreads to the furniture to the walls. Take your pick of suites with sleigh beds or canopied four posters. $$$.

The Stanton House. 76 Maple Ave., Greenwich; (203) 869-2110. Tycoon Stanford White once owned this new century manse. Today, visitors come to stay in the house White slept in. The 21-room hotel mixes old-school charm with modern comforts. Each room features restored furnishings, country-charm quilts and bedspreads and tons of light. The standard rooms are sizable but it's the suites that are a delight, especially the north and south king suites with their sizable living areas, hardwood floors and airy atmosphere. The inn has an outdoor swimming pool and directs guests to area activities. $$$.

new haven

Settled by Puritans in 1638, New Haven became a major trade port between England and America. That didn't last long as New York and Boston superceded New Haven's importance. Nonetheless, the city's economy surged during and after the Civil War as its population soared. The city has been on an upswing, with businesses opening shop and the harbor front and historic districts seeing revitalization. Culture and the arts are strong here, thanks, of course, to Yale University.

getting here

From New York, Metro-North is about an hour and 50 minutes to New Haven (from Greenwich it's about an hour). Take US 1 N and take I-95 N to the Connecticut Turnpike. Connect to CT 34 E toward New Haven (exit 47). Continue onto North Frontage Road. Take a right on Church Street.

where to go

Yale University. Established in 1701, Yale is the focal point of New Haven. Steeped in history and beauty, you can spend days touring the campus and exploring the many museums and cultural opportunities. Start at the **Visitor's Center** (149 Elm St.; 203-432-2300; www .yale.edu/visitor/index.html) where you can peruse exhibits tracing Yale's history. Guided tours of the campus begin at the center and are available Mon through Fri at 10:30 a.m. and 2 p.m., Sat and Sun at 1:30 p.m. Maps for self-guided tours are available, as well, or you can download an audio tour to your MP3 player from www.yale.edu/visitor/mp3tour.html.

Yale University Art Gallery. 1111 Chapel St., New Haven; (203) 432-0600; http://art gallery.yale.edu. As you can well imagine, as one of the world's premier universities, the permanent location is vast and extremely varied and includes antiquities as well as modern pieces. See the website for current exhibits and exhibitions. Open Tues through Sat from 10 a.m. to 5 p.m. (until 8 p.m. on Thurs) and Sun from 1 to 6 p.m. Closed Monday. Admission is free.

Yale Center for British Art. 1080 Chapel St., New Haven; (203) 432-2800; http://ycba .yale.edu/index.asp. The Museum is home to the most expansive collection of British Art outside of the United Kingdom. Open Tues through Sat from 10 a.m. to 5 p.m., and Sun noon to 5 p.m. Closed Monday. Admission is free.

Peabody Museum of Natural History. Science Hill at Yale University; (203) 432-5050; www.peabody.yale.edu. A world-class museum at a world-class university. Founded in 1866, the Peabody showcases the earth's history and is committed to protecting biological diversity. Permanent exhibitions feature dinosaurs—America's premier paleontologist O.C. March was the founder's nephew and instrumental in the dinosaur wing—minerals, space anomalies, reptiles and ancient Egypt, among other attractions. The museum also features touring exhibitions throughout the year. Open 7 days a week. Free admission on Thurs from 2 to 5 p.m. Sept to June. Other days $9 adults, $5 children.

where to shop

Archetype Clothing. 265 College St., New Haven; (203) 562-6772. Located across from Yale University, Archetype Clothing melds modern designs with classic fabrics. The small shop carries some well-known designers—Trina Turk, Theory—but prides itself on helping

legendary long wharf

*The **Long Wharf Theatre** (222 Sargent Dr., New Haven; 203-787-4282; www .longwharf.org) is one of the most prestigious regional theaters in the country, garnering Tony awards for its productions as well as for its modern theatre. The theatre's inaugural performance of Arthur Miller's* The Crucible *in 1965 brought down the house and heralded a dedication to great theatre and amazing talent. Many Broadway and off-Broadway plays got their start here, including* The Shadow Box *and* The Gin Game. *Schedules vary and shows are mostly at night, but often worth the trip.*

up-and-coming artisans—Vince, Ali Ro. Prices are steep—this is designer boutique after all—but you can sometimes score a find that's not going to break the bank.

Atticus Bookstore/Cafe. 1082 Chapel St., New Haven; (203) 776-4040; http://atticus bookstorecafe.com. Located across from the Yale Art Gallery in the Center for British Art's building (it's not part of the museum—you enter on Chapel Street). Opened in 1975, it still has that 70s feel. Buy a book and then jockey with the locals and Yalies alike for a seat in the cafe that serves light vegetarian fare (have the black bean soup) and sweets. Open 7 days.

Celtica. 1008 Chapel St., New Haven; (203) 785-8034. Everything Irish and beautiful—Waterford Crystal, sweaters, caps, mittens, walking sticks, teas, jewelry, pottery.

Fashionista Vintage & Variety. 93 Whitney Ave., New Haven; (203) 777-4434. Many urban vintage stores often sell overpriced garbage, but Fashionista Vintage & Variety sells only one-of-a-kind, gently worn clothing and accessories. Customers can choose from everything from Hermes cufflinks to handmade silk ball gowns. Clothes are catalogued beautifully and the selection is quite extensive and unique. The prices may be steep for some, but the selection is worth the price.

J. Press. 262 York St., New Haven; (203) 772-1310; www.jpressonline.com. Yalies and Connecticut preppies have flocked to J. Press for decades. The store has four locations around the country, but the New Haven store may be the most quintessentially New England of them all. From sport coats to blazers to ties, ascots and trousers, J. Press has everything you need to get to be inducted into Yale's Skulls. Although pricey, J. Press often presents sales with items more than 25 percent off.

Tracy B. 1042 Chapel St., New Haven; (203) 772-2205. Situated in New Haven's historic Chapel Hill area, Tracy B is an eco-friendly women's boutique—clothing, shoes, handbags and jewelry—that brings out your inner fashionista. Designers featured include Graham &

Spencer, LunAlba, Modaspia and Prairie Underground. The selection changes depending on the season. Tracy B often hosts trunk shows during which customers can get discounts on the featured designer's clothing. Prices are a bit steep but sales occur often and everything has a unique feel to it.

The Yale Bookstore. 77 Broadway at York Square, New Haven; (203) 777-8440; http://yale.bncollege.com. Run by Barnes & Noble, if you haven't been to an Ivy League bookstore you should—this one sits at more than 40,000 square feet. There is a floor of books with categories you'd find in any Barnes & Noble, and then there is the educational category where you can find a book on almost any topic. The store also carries Yale apparel and gifts, cosmetics, dorm room necessities, things that are just too unique and funky not to have in your house (at one time they had palm-size wind-up robots), and supplies.

where to eat

Caseus Fromagerie & Bistro. 93 Whitney Ave., New Haven; (203) 624-3373 (203-6-CHEESE); http://caseusnewhaven.com. For many, there's no such thing as consuming too much cheese. Caseus Fromagerie & Bistro owner Jason Sobocinski is a devout follower of this motto, as is evident on his menu at this favorite local eatery, which is open for lunch and dinner. Caseus prides itself on serving locally-grown and locally-produced artisanal delights (the menu will vary by season because of this). This cheese lover's haven offers a variety of cheesy (and noncheesy, for those who prefer moderation) dishes, from small plates and sandwiches like *Poutine* and the famous Grilled Cheese (which boasts up to six different cheeses, depending on the season) to larger plates like the Caseus Wellington and the Mac 'n Cheese (try the onion soup gratin with cheeses from their own shop melted lovingly on top—it'll be the best you've ever had). As an added bonus, Caseus houses a full-service Cheese Shop where one can buy favorite artisanal cheeses and meats. $$.

Claire's Corner Copia. 1000 Chapel St., New Haven; (203) 562-3888. Vegetarians used to have a hard time finding food when they traveled. But thanks to the slow food and organic movement, more vegetarian and vegan eateries are popping up around the country. Clair's Corner Copia may be one of the best even if it's not one of the newest. Since 1975, locals have flocked here and owner Claire Criscuolo has written several books about vegetarian cooking. The all-day menu offers a wealth of good food. From organic tofu rancheros (sans the eggs) to barbecue soy chicken to elaborate veggie burgers and eggplant dishes. The restaurant recently created a gluten-free menu. The gluten-free macaroons are stupendous. $$.

Ibiza. 39 High St., New Haven; (203) 865-1933. This cozy Spanish restaurant, named for the hedonistic Balearic island off its coast, takes classic cuisine and puts an innovative spin on it. Guests can enjoy tapas at the bar and the full menu at small tables centered around

no matter how you slice it . . .

You can't leave New Haven without trying a slice (or several) of the city's signature thin-crust style "apizza"—the only trouble is deciding whose is the best—a problem locals debate about to this day!

Start by heading down to Wooster Street in New Haven's own "Little Italy," a section of town dominated by a family rivalry decades in the making. Stop in at 157 Wooster St. at **Frank Pepe Pizzeria Napoletana** *(203-865-5762; www.pepes pizzeria.com), the originator of New Haven–style pizza. Founded in 1925 by Italian immigrant Frank Pepe, "Pepe's," as it's affectionately known by the locals, has been cooking up some of the nation's best pies in their signature coal-fired bread ovens for generations. The result is what's come to be known as the New Haven style: a thin crust with a slight char, a bit crunchy on the bottom but soft and chewy on top. Still owned today by the Pepe family, don't leave Pepe's without sampling their Signature White Clam Pizza, a Wooster Street staple. Pepe's is open Mon through Sat from 11:30 a.m. to 10 p.m., Sun noon to 10 p.m.*

Of course, it takes two to tango, and **Sally's Apizza,** *located at 237 Wooster St., continues to keep it all in the family. After learning the art of pizza-making from his uncle Frank, in 1938 Salvatore Consiglio decided to break ties and open up his own shop just down the street. Sally's churns out the same style of pizza as its older relative, but some say Sally's has Pepe's beat in their veggie pizza offerings. Sally's is open Tues through Sat from 5 to 10:30 p.m., until 10 p.m. on Sun. Closed Monday. Cash only.*

Which place produces the better pie? You'll have to decide for yourself—just be prepared for a long wait in line outside either establishment. It's a small price to pay to sample some of the world's best pizza.

a warm decor. Try the grilled branzino with Basque rice, or boneless Vermont quail in a roasted vinegar sauce. Every Tuesday patrons are treated to an extensive paella menu— some are traditional, but other offerings mix rice and seafood with things you'd never think of. $$$.

Kudeta. 27 Temple St., New Haven; (203) 562-8844. Downtown New Haven needed a solid Asian eatery and they got it in Kudeta. The restaurant is decorated in golden hues from the banquettes to the lights. The dinner menu showcases a variety of Asian staples from different countries across South and Southeast Asia. You might be impressed by the Sri Lanka crab with asparagus and corn, or the traditional Indonesian salad "Gado Gado"—steamed veggies with tofu and a tangy peanut sauce. But the dry shredded beef with baby bok choy and the Indonesian Rendang beef stew lures the customers again and again. Not everything is meat-centric; Kudeta does serve some vegetarian dishes as well. $$$.

Louis' Lunch. 261–263 Crown St., New Haven; (203) 562-5507; www.louislunch.com. "The Birthplace of the Hamburger Sandwich," this iconic New Haven institution was established in 1895 and has been serving up burgers since 1900 when Louis Lassen invented the hamburger (this is not up for debate with the Lassen family, who still run the restaurant). Louis' is located in the original building—you'll feel like you've stepped back in time. Burgers are cooked in the original cast iron grills and served on toast. Condiments are not allowed—that's right, no ketchup—but you won't need any or miss it. Order the works—that is, onion and tomato, ask for it with cheese (a delicious liquid blend spread on the sandwich), grab a soda, perhaps some potato salad, and a bag of chips. Open Tues through Wed from 11 a.m. to 3:45 p.m., and Thurs through Sat noon to 2 a.m. Closed Sun and Mon. Cash only. $.

Union League Cafe. 1032 Chapel St., New Haven; (203) 562-6712. The *New York Times* has called it "extraordinary," and after having a meal at this chic French restaurant, you'll be looking for even more elaborate superlatives. Union League Cafe has won several awards for effectively marrying French traditional cooking methods with modern techniques. Chef Jean Pierre Vuillermet utilizes local and organic produce and meats to craft wondrous dishes, such as red wine-poached Nova Scotia lobster and roasted organic chicken with summer truffles and mousseline potatoes. The ambiance is at once elegant and inviting with a staff that is eager to please. Closed Sunday and Holidays. $$$$.

where to stay

Farnam Guest House. 616 Prospect St., New Haven; (203) 562-2843; www.farnamguest house.com. Situated less than 2 miles from the Yale campus, Farnam Guest House is a charming Georgian manse that feels like a home away from home. There are 7 rooms available to guests, each with its own style. Rooms are large by bed-and-breakfast standards, with ample space to move about on the hardwood floors. The Farnham room is the most lavish, with a king featherbed, goose down comforter and a twin day bed with trundle. Guests are treated to many amenities, from complimentary newspapers to free Wi-Fi to guest-use kitchen and laundry facilities. $$.

New Haven Hotel. 229 George St., New Haven; (203) 498-3100; www.newhavenhotel .com. This downtown hotel has been recently renovated, thankfully. Everything has been updated, from the lobby to the rooms to the business fitness centers. The rooms and suites are appointed with modern furnishings in neutral tones. Standard rooms have custom-designed dark wood furniture, roman shades and high thread count sheets. Suites have living and dining areas, large kitchens and king beds. Bathrooms feature marble and granite and Grohe fixtures. The hotel offers seasonal specials throughout the year. $$$.

The Study at Yale. 1157 Chapel St., New Haven; (203) 503-3900. Located on Yale University's Arts Campus, The Study at Yale is a unique property not simply for its location. The modern and chic hotel makes guests feel as if they are part of the university. The 124 rooms include 8 "studies" and a presidential suite. Rooms are lofty, with pale blue and white walls, striped carpets, leather chairs and ottomans. Standard rooms have featherbeds enveloped in Frette linens and baths with glass-enclosed showers and marble floors. Studies feature king beds, a book-filled den and views of the campus. The presidential suite is lavish. It has the same blue and neutral theme but has an additional pullout sofa, reading alcove and bath with a deep tub and separate shower. Guests can dine at Heirloom restaurant, on-site, and exercise at a state-of-the-art exercise room. $$$.

Touch of Ireland Guest House. 670 Whitney Ave., New Haven; (203) 787-7997; www .touchofirelandguesthouse.com. Just a small distance from Yale University, Touch of Ireland Guest House evokes memories of classic Irish bed-and-breakfasts. Nestled on several acres, the colonial home offers 4 cute and cozy rooms, 2 named for Irish towns, 2 for relatives of the owners. The Limerick Room is quite possibly the loveliest of the bunch. The dark rose walls, iron bed and view of the gardens evoke a sense of calm. $$.

day trip 03

northeast

of country lanes & the spice trade:
wethersfield, connecticut
simsbury, connecticut

Connecticut has many towns with charming streets and historic flavor. As you make your way towards Hartford, you'll hit several towns that have the requisite Revolutionary-era landmarks, museums, and quite a bit of bucolic beauty. Farms are still plentiful here and sell their produce at the side of the road. Wethersfield is the first of two special towns. It's considered by locals to be the first town incorporated into the state (although that's up for debate). Town planners have managed to keep the historic charm and environmental beauty intact. Simsbury offers lovely parks and a charming historic district. Like Wethersfield, the town has a special kind of pastoral beauty. Town planners are big on green practices.

wethersfield

History and pastoral beauty collide in Wethersfield. Canopies of trees cover country lanes dotted with more than 300 historic homes. History, especially Revolutionary War history is prevalent in Wethersfield. The old quarter downtown, the largest and oldest in the state, boasts 50 homes built *before* the American Revolution. Many of these have been converted into museums to showcase the town's unique past. Thankfully, the town has managed to remain steadfastly colonial despite encroaching development.

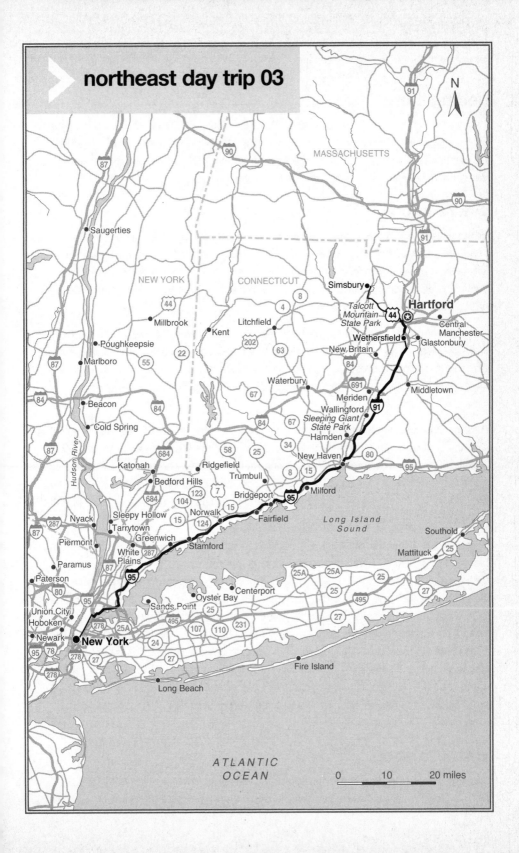

northeast day trip 03

getting there

It's about a 2 hour and 15 minute drive from New York City. Take I-278 East/Bruckner Expressway toward New Haven. Connect to I-95 North/Bruckner Expressway. Take exit 48 for I-91 North toward Hartford. At exit 24 take the right ramp for CT 99 toward Wethersfield/Rocky Hill. Turn right onto CT 99/Silas Deane Highway.

where to go

Captain James Francis House Museum. 120 Hartford Ave., Wethersfield; (860) 529-7656. Operated by the Wethersfield Historical Society, the Captain James Francis House was custom-made by Francis in 1793. The home reflects the differing styles of his descendents. There's a Victorian parlor and a bedchamber in a 1920s style. Open by appointment only.

Cove Warehouse. Cove Park and Main Street, Wethersfield; (860) 529-7161. The Cove Warehouse served as a commercial center at which residents could buy salt, sugar, molasses, and rum from the West Indies. The area traded heavily with the Caribbean, exporting meats, grains, and vegetables. The museum has small exhibits reflecting the importance of the red onion trade to the town.

Hurlbot-Durnham House Museum. 212 Main St., Wethersfield; (860) 529-7161. Another historic home operated by the town's historical society, this Georgian manse was built in the late 1700s and was home to Captain John Hurlbot, a sailor who successfully navigated the globe. A widow and her daughter who married the state's insurance commissioner later occupied it. The Dunhams painted the ceilings and cornices and embellished the walls with rococo revival wallpaper.

Webb-Deane-Stevens Museum. 211 Main St., Wethersfield; (860) 529-0612. A visit to Wethersfield's historic district should always begin at this four-building complex. Three of the buildings abut each other on Main Street. The first is the **Joseph Webb House,** built in 1752, which is the largest of the four. It served as George Washington's war headquarters for a short time and was where Washington planned the military campaign at Yorktown. Visitors can stroll through the Revival Garden out back as well as the Webb Barn. The **Silas Deane House,** built in 1770, was home to a diplomat to France. The **Isaac Stevens House,** built after the war in 1789, showcases many period furnishings as well as a colonial doll exhibit. The last house is a short distance away. The **Buttolph-Williams House,** built in 1715, highlights early Puritan life and was the setting for the Elizabeth George Speare's famous novel, *The Witch of Blackbird Pond.*

where to shop

Clearing House Auction Galleries Inc. 207 Church St., Wethersfield; (860) 529-3344. Many a New Englander heads to estate auctions. Family-owned and operated since the late 1940s, Clearing House hosts estate auctions on Wednesday and Saturday throughout the year. Customers can bid on items while eating pie at the same time. Deals can be had if you are willing to pay the price.

Neill Walsh Goldsmiths and Gallery. 125 Main St., Wethersfield; (860) 721-9256. Neill Walsh has more than 30 years experience working with jewelry. His gallery, which opened in town in 1979, showcases his work, whether traditional or contemporary. Much of the collection has a rustic edge to it with nautical and botanical design elements thrown in.

where to eat

City Fish Market. 884 Silas Dean Hwy., Wethersfield; (860) 522-3129. Since 1930, City Fish Market has been a Wethersfield staple as much for its retail operation as for its dining room. The unpretentious eatery suggests customers order at the counter and eat at comfortable casual seats near the window. The seafood is fresh and prepared without any frills. Just solid food. Lobster is the house specialty, but the soft shell crab and squid are also delicious. $$.

Lucky Lou's Bar & Grill. 222 Main St., Wethersfield; (860) 257-0700. With a massive menu of traditional American fare, Lucky Lou's is one of Wethersfield's favorite eateries. Prices are pretty reasonable considering the area, and the portions are quite substantial. Enjoy a beer or martini while you wait for your South Pacific risotto. $$.

Village Pizza of Wethersfield. 233 Main St., Wethersfield; (860) 563-1513. Village Pizza is a must stop for lunch or dinner and is surprisingly romantic. The pizzeria serves homemade savory Greek-style pizza using quality meats and cheeses. Customers can also order grinders, subs, and calzones as well as some traditional Greek dishes. $$.

where to stay

Chester Bulkley House. 184 Main St., Wethersfield; (860) 563-4236. If you love bed-and-breakfasts, and the over-decoration that often comes with them, you'll love the Chester Bulkley House. Here, every conceivable color in the spectrum can be found inside the Greek Revival home. (One room had so much pink, I thought Barbie had thrown up there.) That's not to say the home is not without its charm. Each of the five rooms is comfortable and has plenty of space. Pine board floors and hand carved balustrades make this a lovely architectural find. And the rates can't be beat for the area. $$.

Silas Robbins House Bed-and-Breakfast. 185 Broad St., Wethersfield; (860) 571-8733. Wethersfield has a number of lodging options but for history and opulence, head to Silas Robbins House Bed-and-Breakfast. Housed in a beautiful Victorian manse, the five romantic rooms are lovingly decorated with plush bedding, oriental rugs, private baths, and period furniture that harkens back to a quieter time. The hotel offers free Wi-Fi throughout the estate. The innkeepers restored the estate during a six-year stretch from 2001 to 2007. $$.

simsbury

Sandwiched between Hartford, Connecticut, and Springfield, Massachusetts, one would think Simsbury would be another example of suburban sprawl gone awry. That's not the case. Despite land in neighboring towns dwindling to make way for wafer-thin houses, Simsbury has managed to avoid the suburbanization, thanks to concerned citizens who want to preserve its charm. Undoubtedly it's changed since its founding in 1670, but it manages to retain a lot of the pastoral beauty that lured English settlers to the area.

getting there

Take US 5 N from Wethersfield to I-91 North to Hartford. At exit 32B take Trumbull Street to US 44/Albany Avenue/Main Street north towards Simsbury. Connect to CT 189 N. Connect to CT 185/Simsbury Road. Take a right on US 202/Hopmeadow Street, which will take you right into town. It's about a 30-minute drive, in the best conditions.

where to go

Heublein Tower. CT 185, Simsbury; (860) 677-0662. Nestled in Talcott Mountain State Park, the Heublein Tower is also a local landmark that deserves mention. Built in 1914 as a summer retreat for a German-born hotelier, the six-storied structure has the best views of the valley and is a great destination for people who like to hike.

Phelps Tavern Museum & Homestead. 800 Hopmeadow St., Simsbury; (860) 658-2500. Operated by the Simsbury Historical Society, this 2-acre site has more than a dozen buildings of historical significance to the town. All tours should start at **Phelps Tavern,** which housed five generations of the Phelps family for almost 200 years. Other buildings at the site include the relocated **Probate Court;** the Queen Anne-style **Carriage House,** ca. 1885; the **School House,** built in 1790; and the gambrel-roofed **Hendricks Cottage,** ca. 1790.

Rosedale Farms & Vineyard. 25 East Weatogue St., Simsbury; (860) 651-3926. Much of the area surrounding Simsbury is a farming community, and Rosedale Farms is considered one of the best farms in the state. The 90-year-old operation provides fresh produce, wine, and flowers, all grown on the premises. The farm is open year-round and hosts special seasonal events including hayrides, wine tastings, chef-to-farm dinners, and corn mazes.

where to eat

Abigail's Grille and Wine Bar. 4 Hartford Rd., Simsbury; (860) 264-1580. Housed in a historic Revolutionary War–era tavern—George Washington and John Adams are said to have stayed here—Abigail's serves delicious food in an elegant setting. The fare runs classic New England with a bit of Italian and Asian-inspired dishes as well. Prices are reasonable and the service is friendly without being obsequious. The tavern is rumored to be haunted by the ghost of Abigail Pettibone who is said to have been murdered by her husband in a jealous rage. $$.

Metro Bis. 928 Hopmeadow Rd., Simsbury; (860) 651-1908. Walk though the Paris Metro train doors and you'll find a classic French bistro that serves up some of the best food in town. Metro Bis is an elegant eatery that caters to anyone wanting an innovative take on classic bistro fare. The affordable 4-course tasting menu is worth the $50 price tag. But the a la carte choices are diverse and interesting enough to keep your palate satisfied. $$$.

Plan B Burger Bar. 4 Railroad St., Simsbury; (860) 658-4477. When you're on the road, sometimes you just crave a burger and a beer. Plan B Burger Bar is the answer to your prayers. The bar serves only free-range, natural angus beef and certified craft beer. The sustainability factor is extended to its other menu items: from boutique Bourbons to mac 'n cheese to its fried mozzarella in basil cream. $$.

where to stay

Simsbury 1820 House. 731 Hopmeadow St., Simsbury; (860) 658-7658. Set on land that once belonged to Revolutionary War hero Noah Phelps, Simsbury 1820 House was built on a hill overlooking the pastoral landscape. It was home to the Phelps family and their descendants, many of which became U.S. Senators and Governors until 1985 when the home was purchased and restored by the Simsbury House Association. The country manor has 32 spacious rooms and suites, all with 19th-century antiques, Belgian linens, and four-posted beds. The inn is pet friendly but charges an additional fee for cleaning and boarding. $$$.

Simsbury Inn. 397 Hopmeadow St., Simsbury; (860) 651-5700. Most lodgings in these small towns are of the bed-and-breakfast variety but The Simsbury Inn is a graceful, large property with plenty of room for groups and families. The 100 rooms and suites feature Provincial decor, with sunny yellow and pale blue getting the most color play. Each of the beds, whether four-poster or sleigh, feature Frette linens and goose down comforters that you can lose yourself in. Some rooms have canopied beds. Definitely opt for those. The hotel offers in-room spa services as well as a restaurant, lounge, and casual cafe. $$$.

northwest

>>>

day trip 01

northwest

>>> **sculpture in the park:**
warwick, new york
mountainville, new york

Most of the communities within a 2-hour drive of New York City offer a wealth of shopping and dining establishments, and hitting them all in a day can be exhausting. For a more sedate day trip, head up the Wawayanda River and further onto NY 32. Breath in the clean air as you drive on the lonely country roads that dot the landscape. Warwick and Mountainville are tiny communities that don't have much to offer in terms of food and lodging. What they lack in a historic downtown they make up for in the outdoor sculpture galleries found in both towns. Art aficionados head here in the hundreds during the summer.

warwick

Warwick isn't much of a town. You won't find high-end shops or locavore eateries. That's OK. You're not coming here for that. It's the wide-open vistas that attract. One can hear the breeze whistling through the trees. It's a place to get back to nature and reflect.

getting there

Take I-87 N to exit 15A/Suffern/Sloatsburg. Turn left onto NY 17 N and then left again on NY 17A. It's about an hour and 30 minutes from New York City.

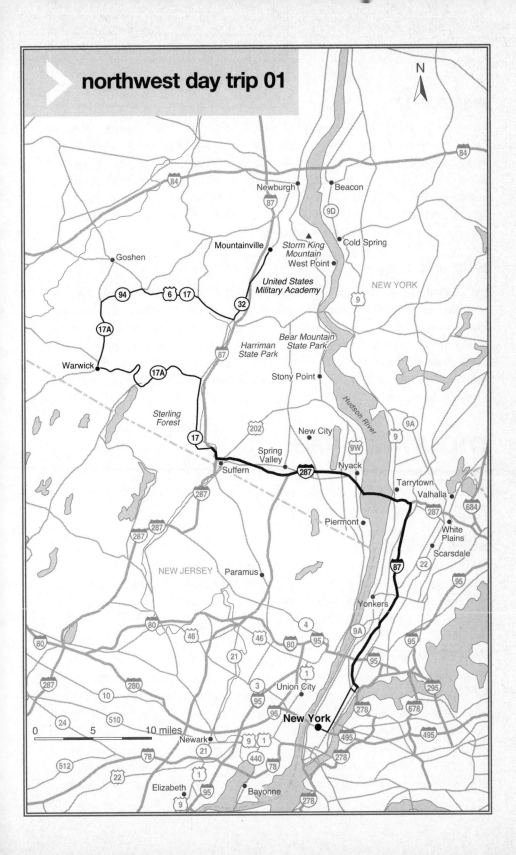

where to go

Pacem in Terris. 96 Covered Bridge Rd., Warwick; (845) 987-9968. Meaning "Peace on Earth," this 6-acre sculpture gallery was created by Dutch-born artist Frederick Franck. Two green spaces house more than 70 large sculptures—made of steel, stone, and wood—some depicting the human form, not all in tranquil poses. Visitors stroll through the walkways quietly and contemplatively. The site has numerous benches carved into trees at which to sit as well as a chapel to reflect further. A small gallery is onsite as well, showcasing drawings and other work by the late artist.

where to stay

Inn at Stony Creek. 34 Spanktown Rd., Warwick; (845) 986-3660. After a day touring Pacem in Terris, wind down at this intimate restored colonial farmhouse. Situated on nine verdant acres, the Inn at Stony Creek has 5 patriotic-themed rooms with rich details and furnishings. The Fox & Hound Suite is the best for letting the bed dominate the room (although the wallpaper is fairly elaborate). Stoneware ewers sit on dressers. It's a throwback to a simpler time. Each room has an en suite bathroom with signature Inn at Stony Creek products. $$$.

mountainville

Much like Warwick, quiet Mountainville stays that way most of the year. That changes in summer when tourist hoards head to the 500-acre sculpture gallery on Storm King Mountain, which seamlessly weaves nature and art.

getting there

From Warwick, it's a 36-minute drive to Mountainville. Head north on NY 17A and bear right onto NY 94 until you see NY 17. Stay on NY 17 until exit 131. Take the ramp for NY 32 toward Suffern/Newburgh. Stay on NY 32 until you see Industry Road. Take a left and you're in Mountainville.

where to go

Storm King Arts Center. Old Pleasant Hill Road, Mountainville; (845) 534-3115. Fusing art and nature. That's what Storm King Arts Center is about. The expansive park boasts hundreds of modern steel sculptures from artists around the world. You can walk through the woods or landscaped lawns and come upon a sculpture without expecting to. It's always a surprise. David Smith's works are the heart and soul of the center—he has 13 on display—but other world-renowned post-war sculptors are represented as well. Some of the work has an earthy feel to it while others are abstract and surreal. The park allows visitors to picnic on the grounds and bikes are for rent. Disabled visitors can get access to the entire facility via trams.

where to eat

Canterbury Brook Inn. 331 Main St., Cornwall; (845) 534-9658. This upscale restaurant offers a dramatic setting at which to enjoy traditional Swiss fare. The views from the dining rooms overlook Canterbury Brook. During the winter, the fireplaces melt the ice, and the exceptional food and service warm the soul. $$$.

Painter's Tavern. 266 Hudson St., Cornwall; (845) 534-2109. Housed in a historic home in the village square, this rustic tavern is a local favorite for its friendly atmosphere and eclectic blend of cuisine, from Italian to Mexican to American. The walls are covered with paintings by local artists, and the bar is teeming with life every day of the week. $$.

where to stay

Storm King Lodge. 100 Pleasant Hill Rd., Mountainville; (845) 534-9421. Located in the shadow of the mountain, Storm King Lodge is a lovely, rustic home run by Hal and Gay Janks that takes you back to the elegance of the 1800s. The lodge has four accommodations, each with beautiful views, private baths, and a homey feel. The lodge also has a private cottage that overlooks the lodge's pool and offers an additional two suites. $$.

day trip 02

northwest

romance in the catskills:
port jervis, new york
barryville, new york

Towns built on romance and peaceful reflection are hard to come by. Head up NY 97, a scenic byway that intersects parts of New York and Pennsylvania, anytime of year for romantic strolls and cozes by the firelight. The Minisink Valley straddles three states and has several quaint towns. Port Jervis and Barryville are both situated at the head of the byway and thankfully haven't been built up. You won't see much around this section of the Delaware River except bubbling brooks, bald eagles, and trees whistling in the breeze.

port jervis

Situated at the beginning of the beautiful Upper Delaware Scenic Byway, a 77-mile-long road built on the remains of the D&H Canal that traverses along the Delaware River, Port Jervis can't help its position as a romantic hamlet. Its friendly locals and cozy restaurants only cement its reputation. Elks-Brox Park is on the mountain and has great overlooks of the tri-state area.

getting there

Take I-95 North to Clifton. Take the ramp to I-80 W towards Hackensack. At exit 64A, take the ramp for NY 17 North. At exit 16, take the ramp to NY 17 West. At exit 121W take I-84 West towards Port Jervis. Take exit 1 to Port Jervis. It takes about an hour and 30 minutes in good traffic.

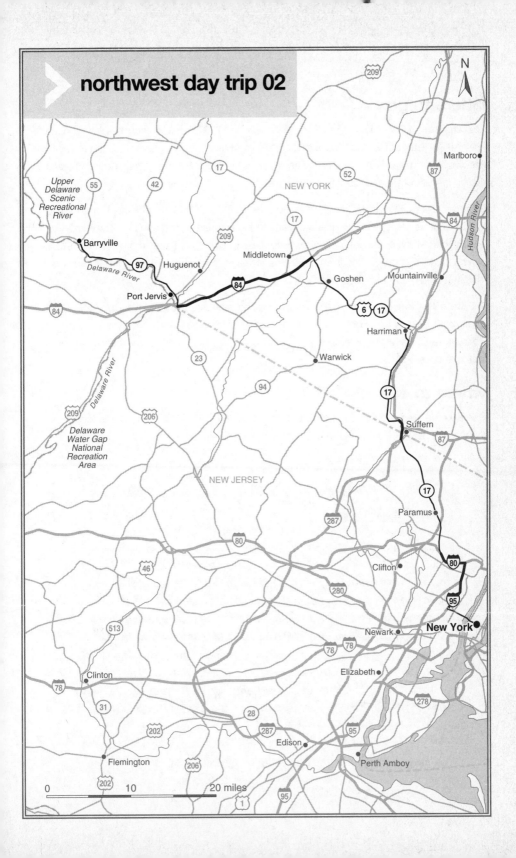

northwest day trip 02

where to go

Fort Decker. 127 West Main St., Port Jervis. Built in 1793, this stone house is listed on the National Register of Historic Places and once served as the headquarters of John B. Jervis (for whom the town is named) and was also a canal hotel for many years. Jervis helped design the Delaware and Hudson Canal.

Gillinder Glass. Erie and Liberty Street, Port Jervis; (845) 856-5375. Gillinder Glass formed in 1861 and is still one of the leading glass manufacturers in the country. The family-run factory specializes in bespoke hand-pressed glass of all colors. Examples of Gillinder Glass can be found in at the Smithsonian's National Museum of American History, the Philadelphia Museum of Art, and the Library of Congress.

Tri-State Rock. Port Jervis. Head up this granite monument that serves as the apex of three state lines—New York, New Jersey, and Pennsylvania—and the confluence of the Delaware and Neversink Rivers. If you stand on the bronze marker you can be in three states at once.

where to eat

Cornucopia Restaurant. 175 US 209, Port Jervis; (845) 856-5361. The Cornucopia Restaurant has been a Port Jervis icon for more than 30 years serving hearty German cuisine.

enjoy the silence

*While traveling to Port Jervis, many visitors come upon what they think is a beautiful Buddhist Monastery. Unfortunately, it's just a Falun Gong temple, closed to the public and patrolled for trespassers (Falun Gong are a cult persecuted in China for their "meditative" practices). Never fear, upstate New York is home to a number of Buddhist shrines and retreats. There's **Sky Lake Lodge** (http:// skylake.shambhala.org) in Rosendale, **Blue Cliff Monastery** (www.bluecliff monastery.org) in Pine Bush, and **Tsechen Kunchab Ling** (www.sakyatemple .org), in Walden, which is 50 percent complete. But the most welcoming and easiest to get to via public transit is the **Dharma Drum Retreat Center** (www .dharmadrumretreat.org) in Pine Bush. This 125-acre retreat is situated on lovely woodland with a peaceful tributary weaving through the trees and meadowlands. Guests sign up for 7- to 10-day retreats during which participants meditate and contemplate life in silence. The Dharma Drum Retreat Center follows the Chan Buddhist path, one of two schools of the Mahayanan branch.*

Locals head here as much for the food as the friendly atmosphere and German beer list. Prices are reasonable. Dinner only. $$.

Erie Hotel and Family Restaurant. 9 Jersey Ave., Port Jervis; (845) 858-4100. Looking for a quick nosh? Head to the Erie Hotel and Family restaurant. The historic eatery serves solid pub fare such as broiled salmon and prime rib in a homey setting. Open seven days a week for lunch and dinner. $$.

where to stay

Sanivan Holistic Retreat & Spa. 12 Columbia Dr., Hurleyville; (845) 434-1849. Port Jervis has no lodging options so you have to head elsewhere. If you really want to get away from it all, head 35 minutes north toward Monticello to the small town of Hurleyville. Here you'll find a bed-and-breakfast with your health and soul in mind. Sanivan Holistic Retreat & Spa is run by a friendly couple that offers guests a choice of three quaint and colorful rooms. Not only do they provide breakfast, but the owners cook you an organic and meat-free lunch and dinner every day of your stay and offer one free facial or massage. The home has a large indoor swimming pool as well as a small sauna. $$$.

barryville

Pristine river views, waterfalls, rock formations, and bald eagles soaring overhead. Barryville beacons with its natural beauty. So much so that John F. Kennedy, Bette Davis, and Paul Newman all have escaped the urban jungle to witness the majestic landscape for themselves. But there is more to tiny Barryville than scenic spots. The town offers a number of charming shops and restaurants at which to enjoy a romantic getaway.

getting there

From Port Jervis, take NY 97 west until you reach Barryville. A yellow flashing light signals your arrival. It's about 20 minutes in good traffic.

where to go

Eagle Institute. NY 97, Lackawaxen, Pennsylvania; (845) 557-6162. Dedicated to protecting our national bird and other birds of prey as well as their natural habitats, Eagle Institute is a nonprofit organization that sponsors guided field trips and lectures on eagle etiquette throughout the winter. Eagle watch weekends occur from January through March with guided excursions on select days.

Minisink Battleground Park. NY 97. Everyone knows about the Battle of Bunker Hill but few know of The Battle at Minisink Ford. On July 22, 1779, nearly 50 militiamen from New York and New Jersey lost their lives. The battle was one of the bloodiest of the Revolutionary

War since it reverberated through the Delaware River communities. General John Sullivan was sent by George Washington to drive British Colonel and Iroquois Chief Joseph Brant out of the area. The park is located four miles north of Barryville. Open Mother's Day to Columbus Day.

Zane Grey Museum. 274 River Rd., Beach Lake, Pennsylvania; (570) 685-4871. Located in nearby Beach Lake, Pennsylvania, this clapboard, 2-story house was the famous writer's home for 13 years in the early part of the 20th century. Grey is best known for novels of an idealized view of the old west. This farmhouse is now a museum that displays Grey's family photos, artifacts, and books. Open from Memorial Day to Labor Day.

where to shop

Barryville Sportsman. 3461 NY 97, Barryville; (845) 557-9907. The upper Delaware region is replete with great fishing and hunting sites and Barryville Sportsman equips many of the area's outdoors enthusiasts. The Sportsman carries live bait, flies, tackle, ammo, guns, and ice fishing gear. The store also hosts hunting safety courses for novice hunters.

Bluestone Pottery. 159 Rio Dam Rd., Glen Spey, New York; (845) 856-7398. Owner Kim Lust creates handmade mugs, bowls, casserole dishes, pots, and other items at her small studio 5 miles south of Barryville. Lust works with a 50-cubic-foot kiln in her studio and produces items that are microwave and dishwasher safe.

where to eat

Carriage House. 3351 NY 97, Barryville; (845) 557-0400. If you miss grandma's home cooking never fear. The Carriage House creates dishes that will fill the void. Built in the early 20th century, the landmark restaurant serves homemade bread and continental dishes at its dining room, grill/bar area, and outdoor patio. Some showcase the area's German roots but most are familiar to American palates. Prices are reasonable and a children's menu is available for anyone under 12. Open seven days a week for lunch and dinner. $$.

where to stay

Ecce. 19 Silverfish Rd., Barryville; (845) 557-8562. Surprisingly, Barryville has several decent lodging options but nothing beats the stark beauty and elegance of Ecce. The bed-and-breakfast sits on 60 wooded acres on a bluff overlooking the Delaware River. The views are spectacular. Guests have a choice of 5 distinctive rooms, each with TVs, fridges, DVD players and dramatic views of the surrounding land. The inn also has a play room and a sunroom as well as several outdoor decks on which to relax. $$$.

day trip 03

northwest

culinary rockland county:
piermont, new york
nyack, new york

Day-trippers from the city often overlook Rockland County. Heading up NY 9A out of the city, most urbanites veer right at Dobbs Ferry to more popular Westchester County for quick getaways. That's a shame because your dollar goes further on the other side of the Tappan Zee Bridge. Many of the towns lining this side of the rocky Palisades garner no more than a cursory glance as you drive down the winding roads, but both Piermont and Nyack have appeal, especially if you're a gourmand. Witness the burgeoning culinary and art scene first hand at both riverside towns.

piermont

A picturesque river village that was once an important thoroughfare for colonists moving supplies during the Revolutionary War, Piermont has long been in the shadow of its tonier neighbors across the river in Westchester County. That's changing now that Manhattanites have discovered its beautiful riverside restaurants, galleries, shops, and marina. The town is a popular thoroughfare for hardcore bicyclists who race up US 9W during the spring, summer, and early fall.

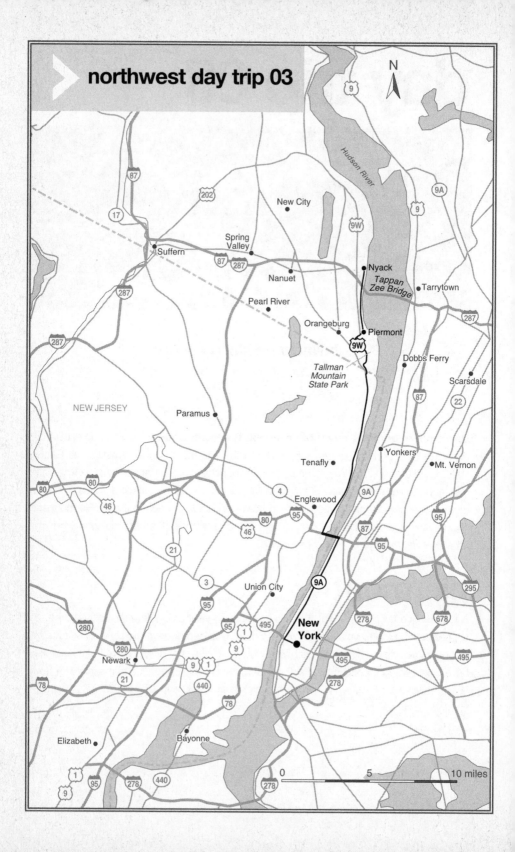

getting there

Rockland Coaches run regular weekday and weekend service via US 9 from the Port Authority Bus Terminal to New City or Stony Point in Rockland County. The trip from the Port Authority to Piermont takes a little more than an hour.

Driving to Piermont is a breeze. Just head up the Henry Hudson Parkway to the George Washington Bridge. Take the Palisades Parkway North and connect to US 9W, which takes you straight into town. The trip should take 45 minutes, not accounting for traffic.

where to go

Onderdonk House. 758 Piermont Ave., Piermont. Home to American patriots and fired upon by British troops during the Revolutionary War—residents preserved cannonballs found on the front lawn—the current structure was built over a 130-year period from 1737 to 1867. The sandstone home has a gabled roof and a one and a half story wing.

where to shop

Buttercup & Friends & Buttercup's Baby. 535 Piermont Ave., Piermont; (845) 359-1669. Buttercup & Friends specializes in beautifully crafted children's clothing and vintage toys. The clothing selection—brands include Robies, Kicky Pants, etc.—uses mostly organic fabrics, and the toys make one feel nostalgic for a bygone era.

Gallery Moderne. 7 Round House Rd., Piermont; (845) 359-4305. This local mainstay specializes in Rene Lalique, from drawings to crystal vases. The gallery also has a number of paintings and modern art pieces on display, mostly from Olivier Raab.

Ki. 510 Piermont Ave., Piermont; (845) 848-2020. Ki specializes in organic and handmade garments, mainly knits, hand-dyed clothing, coats, dresses, and jackets. Many of the items utilize only organic dyes from a variety of natural sources. Brands include OSKA, Iconoclast, and Sarah Pacini.

The Outside In Piermont. 249 Ferndon Ave., Piermont; (845) 398-0706. The Outside boasts an indoor and outdoor collection of crafts as well as fine art and other works by Hudson Valley artists. Much of the collection has a green element to it, with reclaimed and recycled materials used. The gallery also sells soap, candles, jewelry, ceramics, and saw horses. The Outside also does commissioned work by appointment.

Village of Piermont Farmers' Market. Ash Street and Piermont Avenue, Piermont; (845) 359-1258. The town sponsors this farmers' market through the spring until mid-Nov. Customers can shop for local produce, meats, flowers, cheese, wine, and other goods.

> ## a one woman job

New City in Rockland County boasts a green space that was the only Depression-era project supervised and created by a woman. Mary Mowbray-Clarke, a local landscape architect, constructed the Dutch Gardens over a four-year period beginning in 1934. The original gardens sat on 10 acres and featured a teahouse with a brick fireplace and terrace, a bandstand flanked by cedar trees, a black pergola, a gazebo, and numerous beds of flowers and plants including tulips, peonies, roses, Himalayan pine, and Sweet Bay Magnolias. It was so beloved that Eleanor Roosevelt put it on the map by paying it a visit in 1935. Dutch Gardens won numerous landscape design awards in subsequent years by magazines and architecture firms.

Only a small portion of the original site remains due to neglect in the 1970s and '80s. The garden went through extensive renovations during the latter part of the 20th century. You can stroll through the remains of the 2-story teahouse as well as the bandstand and gazebo. The patio is a popular spot on which local residents savor their brown-bag lunch.

where to eat

Freelance Cafe & Wine Bar. 506 Piermont Ave., Piermont; (845) 365-3250. Abutting Xaviar's restaurant, this less formal cafe serves Italian, American, and French favorites. Opened in 1989, chef Peter Kelly has garnered many accolades for his innovative spin dishes such as roasted Hudson Valley duck and Cornish game hen. Open Tues through Sun for lunch and dinner. $$$.

Sidewalk Bistro. 482 Piermont Ave., Piermont; (845) 680-6460. An elegant French bistro that has both comfortable outdoor and indoor seating. The setting is convivial, especially if you are lucky enough to get a seat in the pretty outdoor garden. Enjoy dishes such as the mussels in garlic sauce and soft-shell crabs. $$$.

Slattery's Landing Steakhouse. 5 Roundhouse Rd., Piermont; (845) 398-1943. Overlooking the Hudson River and the Tappan Zee Bridge, Slattery's Landing is a popular eatery that serves quintessential American fare in a refined setting. Locals love the restaurant for its storied Afternoon Tea and prix fixe Sunday brunch. The former is a local tradition. Even little girls get in on the act from 3 to 5 p.m. Open daily throughout the year. $$.

nyack

It means "a point of land." And the Nyack Indians, for which the village is named, enjoyed fishing on this point of land in the Palisades that juts out onto the Hudson River. After Europeans settled the area in the 18th and 19th centuries, the town became home to a sandstone quarry, six shoe factories, four cigar factories, and three shipyards. The Nyack of today is no longer a manufacturing mecca. Instead, it's been imbued with a sense of reinvigoration and historic preservation. The downtown boasts quite a few cultural and culinary institutions that make it worth a day or weekend getaway.

getting there

Take the Rockland Coaches Stony Point or New City bus two stops from Piermont to Nyack. It takes about nine minutes. From Piermont, it's a short drive up the Hudson to Nyack. Take Piermont Avenue straight into Nyack. It's about a 10-minute drive.

where to go

Amazing Grace Circus. www.amazinggracecircus.org. Since 2002, the Amazing Grace Circus has taught area children and teens to juggle, perform on a trapeze, do clown antics, and work puppets like adult circus performers. The children train and perform year-round mostly in a tent in Nyack's Memorial Park and Rockland Country Day School. Children learn confidence-building exercises.

Edward Hopper House Art Center. 82 North Broadway, Nyack; (845) 358-0774. American realist painter Edward Hopper was born and spent much of his childhood in this home, listed on the National Register of Historic Places. In 1971, the 2-story Queen Anne-style home was turned into a gallery space featuring emerging and established artists as well as workshops, lectures, concerts, and figure drawing lessons.

Elmwood Playhouse. 10 Park St., Nyack; (845) 353-1313. This community theater, established in 1947, is housed in a 100-year-old building. The theater has staged more than 300 plays and musicals. It also hosts children's arts classes and workshops.

Nyack Beach State Park. 698 North Broadway, Upper Nyack; (845) 268-3020. The area has a number of nice parks but the Nyack Beach State Park is the nicest of all. Nestled on 61 acres, the park boasts picnic areas, hiking and biking trails, and fishing areas. During the winter, visitors can traverse cross-country trails.

Riverspace. 119 Main St., Nyack; (845) 348-0741. Incorporating the Helen Hayes Youth Theatre, Riverspace is an arts and cultural center that educates and entertains the lower Hudson Valley community. The center hosts theater, dance, music, film performances, and screenings and has featured such illustrious personages as Meryl Streep. The center also runs workshops, internships, and master classes for people of all ages.

where to shop

Antiques Masters. 87 Main St., Nyack; (845) 727-7700. Antiques Masters are just that. The store sells a wide array of European and American antiques, furniture, lamps, chandeliers, tapestries, tea sets, and reproductions. Everything is very high-end. The shop can also be hired to restore and repair priceless heirlooms and to help design your home.

Circa 2000. 13 South Broadway, Nyack; (845) 353-4711. For more than 50 years, Circa 2000 has been specializing in high-end antiques, art, and furniture. The selection is in pristine condition and changes pretty regularly. The shop also deals in custom-made Habersham Furniture.

ML Gifts and Accessories. 75 South Broadway, Nyack; (845) 358-1293. ML Gifts caters to an eco-friendly crowd. Most of the clothing, shoes, jewelry, and bags are environmentally friendly (brands include TOMS shoes and Melie Bianco purses). The store also boasts a good collection of soaps, candles, and other bath and beauty products.

where to eat

Art Cafe of Nyack. 65 South Broadway, Nyack; (845) 353-4230. A truly unique and cozy place to nosh, the Art Cafe serves Middle Eastern inspired American staples from homemade hummus to malawach to toastinis to omelettes. The ambience is homey, making you feel as if you are visiting a friend, and the staff certainly cement this feeling. Open seven days a week for breakfast and lunch. $.

Hudson House. 134 Main St., Nyack; (845) 353-1355. Housed in a former jail, Hudson House is a longtime local favorite. Fish, meat, and pasta dishes are the main draw but the butterscotch pudding entices as well. Make sure to check out the wine cellar, which is located in the building's jail cells. Guests can opt for a $44, 3-course (plus wine tasting) menu. During the summer, diners head to the patio. Open Tues through Sun for lunch and dinner. $$.

Main Essentials. 145 Main St., Nyack; (845) 512-8692. A Caribbean-vegetarian restaurant in an area known for steakhouses. Main Essentials is a welcome addition to Main Street, serving flavorful Caribbean fare. The restaurant's menu showcases meat alternatives—mostly of the seitan variety—as well as rice, beans, yucca, and plantains. Prices are affordable and the staff is extremely friendly. The restaurant also offers a number of vegan options. $.

True Food. 166 Main St., Nyack; (845) 480-5710. Fresh food and made-to-order items. True Food has quickly become a local favorite for its friendly service and commitment to creating great tasting items using quality ingredients. The veggie burger, wheatberry salad, and yucca lasagna have all garnered accolades. The restaurant also has a number of gluten-free options. $$.

southwest

>>>

day trip 01

southwest

the buck stops here:
new hope, pennsylvania
fallsington, pennsylvania

Heading Southwest from the city, you eventually hit historic Bucks County. Georgian and stone manses dot the landscape, and the sun peeks out from trees overhanging winding country lanes. The area has a long and illustrious social and cultural history, from Native American settlements to Germanic towns to New Age meccas. This day trip takes you to two drastically different towns not far from each other. New Hope has an earthy, crunchy vibe much like Woodstock, New York, while nearby Fallsington is caught in a time warp. It's as if it's still 1775.

new hope

Psychics. Herbalists. Mystics. Pennsylvania's answer to Woodstock has them in spades and if you're at all interested in that sort of thing, you'll want to spend more than a day here. New Hope is centered around a single main street that runs along the Delaware River, with shops, restaurants, galleries, bed-and-breakfasts, and a decent theater company. It's a popular destination for motorcyclists who like to line their bikes up main street as if it's a mini-Sturgis. Locals enjoy their proximity to the Delaware, going for boat rides on the river. The shops tend to be anything from crafts to new age emporiums.

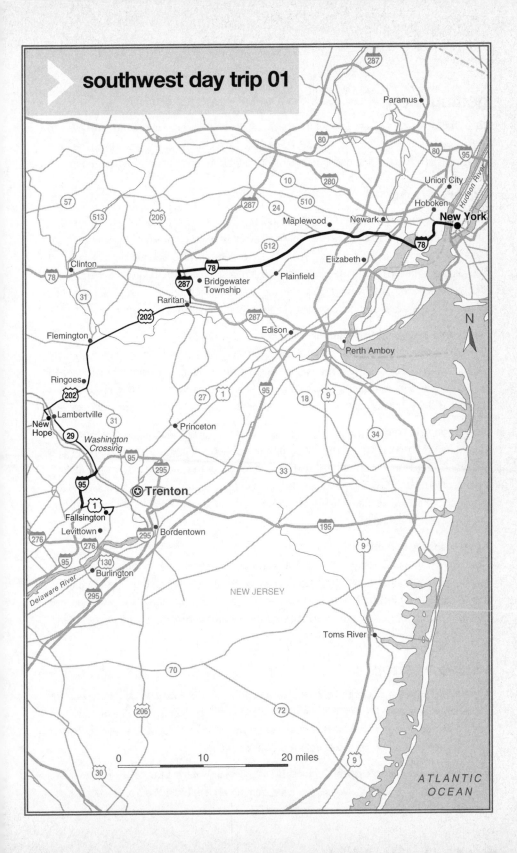

southwest day trip 01

getting there

Take the New Jersey Turnpike South to exit 14/Newark Airport. Head onto I-78 West to I-287 South. Stay on I-287 until you hit US 202 S. Take US 202 S until you reach the New Hope exit, which is the first one in Pennsylvania. It's about an hour and 15-minute trip.

where to go

Bucks County Playhouse. 70 South Main St., New Hope; (215) 862-2046. Housed in what was once a gristmill, the Bucks County Playhouse is one of the most renowned small theater companies in the country. Since 1939, a number of productions have featured famous actors including Grace Kelly, Leslie Nielson, and Walter Matthau. A number of well-known plays have got their start here (*Barefoot in the Park* being just one). The playhouse still stages Broadway-level plays on both its Main Stage and Children's Stage.

New Hope & Ivyland Railroad. 32 West Bridge Rd., New Hope; (215) 862-2332. Head aboard this vintage passenger train that takes you on hour-long scenic rides through quiet sections of Bucks County. The 1920s-era trains are either steam or diesel locomotives, and both have bar cars for guests' enjoyment. The railroad organizes special train excursions throughout the year, including a murder mystery train tour as well as the north pole express.

New Hope Arts Center. 2 Stockton Ave., New Hope; (215) 862-9606. The New Hope Arts Center strives to enrich the cultural lives of area residents through contemporary art and sculpture. The center hosts annual exhibitions throughout the year, including the Works in Wood, which recognizes woodworkers from around the country, and the Indoor and Out-door Sculpture New Hope, which showcases three-dimensional works. Visitors can also take classes and attend lectures.

Parry Mansion Museum. 45 South Main St., New Hope; (215) 862-5652. Home to the New Hope Historical Society, the Parry Mansion was home to the "father of New Hope" and four subsequent generations of his family. Each room boasts furniture and other artifacts from a different period in its history. Docents take guests through the colonial kitchen, the Victorian music room, the child's room, and the federal bedroom. The homestead also features an icehouse as well as a barn.

where to shop

Mystickal Tymes. 127 South Main St., New Hope; (215) 862-5629. A one-stop shop for wiccans and pagans. Mystickal Tymes sells wands, chalices, incense, chakra sets, and scrying mirrors as well as a wealth of other items. The shop also doubles as a fortuneteller, offering tarot card readings and astrological chartings.

Not Too Shabby Chic Crafts, Collectables & Consignment LLC. 26 North Main St., New Hope; (215) 862-7093. Boasting a collection of handcrafted items from local artisans,

Not Too Shabby features a wide array of hand-thrown pottery, woodcrafts, wind chimes, soaps, and other things for the home.

Rice's Market. 6326 Greenhill Rd., New Hope; (215) 297-5993. During the summer, Rice's Market showcases hundreds of vendors from around the area. The 30-acre site boasts antiques, used merchandise, fresh produce, Amish goods, clothing, and other items.

Teardrop Memories. 12 West Mechanic St., New Hope; (215) 862-3401; www.tear dropmemories.com. Teardrop Memories is a shop of oddities. From Victorian mourning jewelry to Georgian human hair wreaths, the shop is not your average antiques store and it's certainly not for the faint of heart. The shop carries curios such as circus paraphernalia, primitive masks, even vintage embalming tables. The shop runs a lucrative website as well.

where to eat

The Landing. 22 North Main St., New Hope; (215) 862-5711. Riverside dining is always a treat at The Landing, the most popular restaurant of its kind in Bucks County. Enjoy regional American fare while dining under an open sky during the summer or by the fire in the winter. Popular menu items include Muffuletta, seared sea scallops, and peppercorn-crusted tuna. The restaurant also features a kids' menu and vegetarian items. $$.

Marcella's North. 7 East Ferry St., New Hope; (215) 862-1700. Situated in one of the oldest buildings in town, Marcella's is one of New Hope's most popular eateries. The restaurant brings in the crowds due to its beautiful ambience—wooden beams and stained glass windows abound—and its seasonal, eclectic menu. Pasta, seafood, and fresh vegetables get top billing. $$.

where to stay

Lexington House. 6171 Upper York Rd., New Hope; (215) 794-0811. Consistently rated as one of the top bed-and-breakfasts in Bucks County, The Lexington House majestically overlooks 4 acres of bucolic property. Visitors give thanks for this as downtown New Hope can get a bit busy, especially during the summer and fall. The colonial home boasts 6 rooms, all antiques-laden, but painstakingly decorated with some modern flourishes. The owners are not afraid of color as one bathroom features a pink vanity and toilet. The estate encompasses a carriage house, a springhouse, smokehouse, and several other historic outbuildings. $$$.

Mansion Inn. 9 South Main St., New Hope; (215) 862-1231. A Baroque Victorian mansion that's been converted into a charming bed-and-breakfast. Mansion Inn has 7 rooms, 5 of which are suites, all of which are individually decorated to reflect the unique history of the property (it was the first home in town to get running water). Four-poster beds, oriental rugs, and floral wallpaper create a welcoming atmosphere. $$.

fallsington

Leaving behind the teeming throngs in New Hope, you'll quickly come across some unwanted development on the river. New condos are ruining the otherwise pristine landscape. Within 20 minutes, the new condos give way to tree-covered, badly paved lanes. You've arrived in Fallsington. It has a drastically different vibe from New Hope. You won't find new age kitsch or a shopper's paradise. Instead, the town is home to more than 90 historic buildings, many of which date back to the 17th century. The historic section of town features stone house after stone house as well as gothic revival homes, fanning out from Meetinghouse Square.

getting there

Head down NJ 29 S from New Hope until you get to I-95 S. Stay on I-95 S until you hit exit 46A. Take the right ramp for US 1 N towards Morrisville. Take the right ramp to Fairless Hills. It's about a 30-minute drive from New Hope.

where to go

Historic Fallsington, Inc. 4 Yardley Ave., Fallsington; (215) 295-6567. Visitors should head here as soon as they get into town. The office has great suggestions on places to visit as well as a walking map that shows the 21 buildings in town that are worth a visit (many are private homes). The most notable of these are **Burges Lippincotts,** which is a 19th-century fieldstone building once home to the village doctor. **The Gambrel Roof House** was the second meetinghouse for the town (the first burned down), built in 1728 and has been home to a female boarding school as well as private apartments. The **William Penn Center–3rd Meetinghouse** served as a Quaker meetinghouse and is now a kindergarten and community center. **The Stagecoach Tavern** was built in 1793 and has served as a watering hole, hotel, lodge hall, and hardware store. **The Moon–Williamson Log House** is one of the oldest still at its original site in the state. Built in the 1760s of dovetailed logs, the home has been restored to its former glory by Historic Fallsington, Inc.

day trip 02

southwest

victorian new jersey:
frenchtown, new jersey
lambertville, new jersey

Quaint and charming can't begin to describe the towns of Frenchtown and Lambertville, both halfway points between New York City and Philadelphia. Both are noted for their Victorian architecture as well as their burgeoning dining and arts scenes. Numerous new businesses have relocated to the area for its natural beauty, tranquil river setting, and position as a popular destination in Hunterdon County. Still, with all the interest and development, both towns are replete with quiet places to unwind and contemplate life.

frenchtown

Frenchtown is a haven for Francophiles who can't get to the real thing (founding father Paul Henri Mallet-Prevost immigrated here during the French Revolution). Nestled in the Delaware Valley at the convergence of two creeks, the charming town showcases a quieter slice of life from cute boutiques and restaurants to meandering bike paths along the river to tranquil fishing spots. The downtown commercial district features many buildings from the Victorian era. Most have been lovingly restored rather than demolished for new development.

getting there

Take NJ 139 W to US 1 S to I-78 W. Take exit 15 to NJ 173 E toward Clinton. Bear left on CR 513. Stay on CR 513, which changes to Race Street until you see Second Street. Take a right.

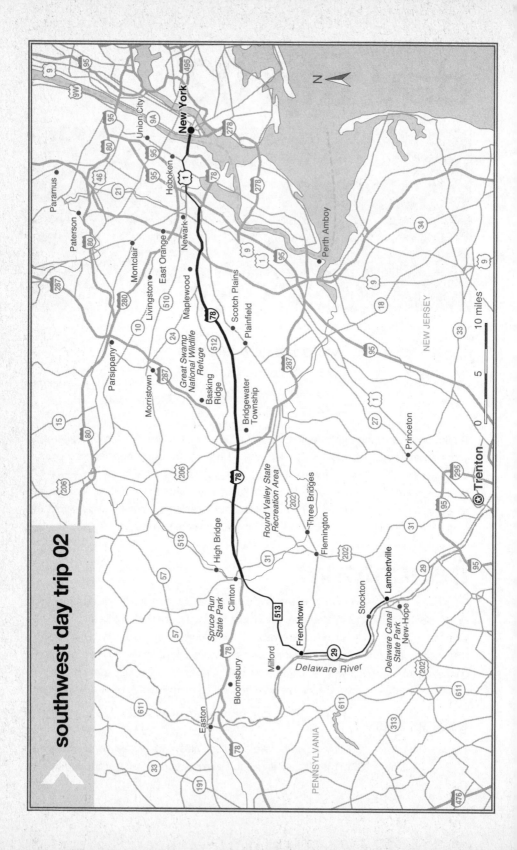

southwest day trip 02

where to go

Kayaking on the River. The area is home to a host of kayak rental shops, most in nearby New Hope or Lambertville. Head to **Paddle Creek** (26 Race St.; 908-996-0000). The shop has a friendly and knowledgeable staff that evaluates your skills and sets you up with the right kayak or canoe for traversing the river (experienced paddlers can opt for white water kayaks).

Poor Richard's Winery. 220 Ridge Rd., Frenchtown; (908) 996-6480. With parachutists and skydivers as a backdrop, this 15-acre winery built into the mountainside creates everything by hand. A deck overlooks the vineyard for relaxing with a glass of wine under the summer sun. The winery specializes in French hybrids and offers a wide selection of whites and reds including Seyval Blanc and Chambourcin.

where to shop

Beasley's Book Bindery. 106 Harrison St., Frenchtown; (908) 996-9993. One of the most unique stores in town, Beasley's helps protect your precious book collection by providing leather covers for fiction or nonfiction. The shop also sells handmade stationery, sketchbooks, and desk sets. Kids will delight in the shop's wide array of pop-up books.

European Country Designs. 39 Bridge St., Frenchtown; (908) 996-7493. European Country Designs specializes in home furnishings in a French provincial style. From the selection of handpainted ceramics to fine bed linens to natural soaps, you know you're getting the real thing there.

Focus on Fiber Art. 10 Bridge St., Frenchtown; (908) 996-3344. Quilter and fiber artist Elena Stokes runs this gallery that showcases her textile art as well as that of other area artists. The gallery also sells a number of mixed media, pottery, metal art, and paintings.

vive la switzerland!

Frenchtown may not seem very French to anyone who's been to the real thing, but for many a tourist, it's the closest they are ever going to get. Thanks to early resident and wealthy landowner Paul Henri Mallet-Prevost, the village adopted the name Frenchtown (area residents thought the Swiss native was French based on the language he spoke. Sacre Bleu!) The Frenchtown of today is drastically different from Mallet's day save for some of the architecture, but one wonders if he'd approve of the little village that loosely resembles a southern French town. Or if he'd make them change it to Swisstown. No, that doesn't have a ring to it.

The Spinnery. 33 Race St., Frenchtown; (908) 996-9004. The Spinnery sells used and antique weaving equipment as well as supplies for weavers and knitters and kits for children. The shop also teaches classes on weaving, knitting, dyeing, and felting.

Thistle. 38 Bridge St., Frenchtown; (908) 996-7080. Thistle features a wide array of home goods, tabletop items, candles, county-style furniture, dishes, and platters. Everything is fairly priced and the selection changes regularly.

where to eat

Blue River Cafe. 51 Bridge St., Frenchtown; (908) 996-8811. Serving breakfast, lunch, and dinner, the Blue River Cafe specializes in inexpensive American cuisine in a friendly and casual setting. Guests can relax on the shaded patio in summer or in the comfortable restaurant during colder months. The menu features the ubiquitous burgers and salads as well as fried shrimp and southern fried chicken. Closed Monday. $.

Bridge Cafe. 8 Bridge St., Frenchtown; (908) 996-6040. Bridge cafe has been a popular eatery long before the tourists came to Frenchtown. Since 1987, the restaurant is housed in Frenchtown's original train depot. You can still see remnants from the structure. The restaurant serves healthy and hearty fare. Locals head here in the morning for coffee. Tourists tend to come in the afternoons for the great river views and reasonably priced menu, with items such as homemade donuts and spinach rice cakes. $$.

where to stay

National Hotel. 31 Race St., Frenchtown; (908) 996-3200. A historic landmark built in 1851, the National Hotel has seen the likes of Annie Oakley and Buffalo Bill Cody. Each of the 10 rooms has comfortable beds and historic flourishes. Some of the rooms have whirlpool baths and private porches. The hotel can organize private, in-room yoga and pilates lessons for guests. The hotel went through an extensive renovation in 2004 to modernize a bit of the interior but kept the historic flavor of the structure intact. $$$.

Widow McCrea House. 53 Kingwood Ave., Frenchtown; (908) 996-4999. Just a stone's throw from downtown Frenchtown is the Widow McCrea House. Heavy on antiques and floral wallpaper, the house caters to an older crowd looking for a romantic getaway. Rooms are divided into three separate accommodations: The main house boasts 3 sizeable rooms with antique beds and furnishings. The Kase Family Cottage is perfect if you want privacy. It comes with a Jacuzzi and in-room dining. The Anne–James Suite and the Privacy Suite have elaborate furnishings as well. The hotel offers last-minute specials as well as off-season discounts. $$$.

lambertville

One of the oldest communities in Hunterdon County, Lambertville has seen its fair share of ups and downs, from its start as a major trading port to the development of the Delaware Raritan canal to its downturn during the Great Depression. Today, Lambertville thrives because of a dedicated and proud populace and its emergence as a culinary and antiques mecca in the northeast.

getting there

From Frenchtown, go on NJ 29 S past a rock wall on one side, trees overhead, and the river on the other side. Once you pass the village square, stone houses, and the entrance to the D&R Canal State Park, you'll hit the antiques shops and galleries on Lambert Street.

where to go

Holcombe-Jimison Farmstead Museum. 1605 Daniel Bray Hwy., Lambertville; (609) 397-2752. The museum preserves the area's agricultural history. Exhibits in the 3-story red bank barn and surrounding outbuildings range from a print shop to a blacksmith shop to a doctor's office. The main home was built in 1711 and has an herb garden and expansive rooms.

James Wilson Marshall House Museum. 60 Bridge St., Lambertville; (609) 397-0770. Home to the Lambertville Historical Society, the James Wilson Marshall House was once home to a cabinet and coach maker and to James Wilson Marshall, who discovered gold prospecting in California. His discovery started the Gold Rush. Built in 1816, the home has been restored with period antiques and houses the historical society's archival collection. It also hosts exhibits about area history including the shad fishing industry, which once spurred the local economy.

where to shop

Hrefna Jonsdottir. 24 Bridge St., Lambertville; (609) 397-3274. This Icelandic gallerist, a Lambertville icon for three decades, sells contemporary art—oils, acrylics, mixed media, etc.—most by local artists as well as a small selection of prints and photographs.

Palette. 63 Bridge St., Lambertville; (609) 397-0101, Several area antiques dealers opened Palette on the first floor of a historic home. If you look hard enough you can find Gucci handbags and vintage designer dresses. House wares, contemporary art, pillows, and painted mirrors abound.

Phoenix Books. 39 North Union St., Lambertville; (609) 397-4960. Spend hours comfortably browsing through this gem. The store boasts a solid selection of critically acclaimed works as well as rare, out-of-print, and used books including fiction, cooking, gardening, and military tomes. Prices are reasonable.

Zinc Home + Garden. 74 Bridge St., Lambertville; (609) 397-5800. Design veterans Rod and Tracey Berkowitz sell high-end furniture, one-of-a-kind antiques, home goods, and crafts at this store new to the Bridge Street scene. A globe lampshade catches the eye as does a green iron bench and antique pencil sharpeners.

where to eat

Bell's Tavern. 183 North Union St., Lambertville; (609) 397-2226. Since 1938, locals and tourists have been frequenting this homey tavern that serves Italian cuisine as well as some American classics. If you're not in the mood to eat, head to the bar and enjoy more than 15 wines by the glass, top-shelf whiskeys, and tequilas. The bar uses the Maxwell Refrigeration System to chill its beer before it's poured. $$.

Sneddon's Luncheonette. 47 Bridge St., Lambertville; (609) 397-3053. This old school luncheonette is unique from others in the area. Nothing is frozen. Everything is homemade, and the menu features an array of familiar dishes such as wraps, salads, and cakes. $.

Station Restaurant. 11 Bridge St., Lambertville; (609) 397-8300. The Station Restaurant boasts a unique setting. It's housed in the 19th-century train station. The restaurant serves regional American cuisine with a twist. Wild game such as elk and grass-fed meats are the focus, with innovative sides and starters. Diners can savor food and wine in the formal dining room as well as the pub and a canal-side outdoor space. $$$.

where to stay

Inn at Lambertville Station. 11 Bridge St., Lambertville; (609) 397-4400. The Inn at Lambertville Station enjoys a great location in the heart of downtown Lambertville. The iconic property, once the local train station, has 45 rooms, fashioned after great cities—Paris, New Orleans, San Francisco, etc. Each room is full of antiques as well as modern amenities (flatscreen TVs, Wi-Fi) with great Delaware River views. Upgrade to the suites, which boast gas fireplaces. The hotel offers Sunday and weekday getaway packages as well as wine country staycations throughout the year. $$$.

Lambertville House. 32 Bridge St., Lambertville; (609) 397-0200. A Victorian manse that attracts tourists from all around. The Lambertville House has 26 charming rooms, each seamlessly blending the modern with the vintage. Rooms have lovely sleigh bed frames, wall-to-wall carpeting, and private baths with marble fixtures. Couples craving more privacy can opt for one of two carriage-house rooms, each with terraces, fridges, and separate rainforest shower. $$.

day trip 03

southwest

>>> **college splendor:**
princeton, new jersey

Ivy-covered buildings, hallowed halls, and knowledge-hungry students. America has a surplus of lovely college towns, some big, some small. Although Boston is filled to the brim with lovely campuses, and towns such as Ann Arbor, Madison, and Berkley often garner accolades for their beauty, Princeton may have them all beat. Is it its proximity to both Philadelphia and New York City? Is it the wonderful examples of architectural styles, from English Vernacular to Georgian to Green Revival to Italianate? Or its pristine setting along the Delaware Raritan Canal? No one can agree. What one does know is that it has a wealth of interesting sites, shops, and eateries and is considered one of the top towns in the United States in which to live and work.

princeton

getting there

From Penn Station, take New Jersey Transit's Northeast Corridor line to Princeton. You have to transfer at Princeton Junction to the Princeton Shuttle to downtown Princeton. The trip takes about 2 and a half hours.

The drive from New York City to Princeton takes just over an hour in the best conditions. Take the Holland Tunnel to I-78 W. Connect to I-95 S. Connect to NJ 18 onto

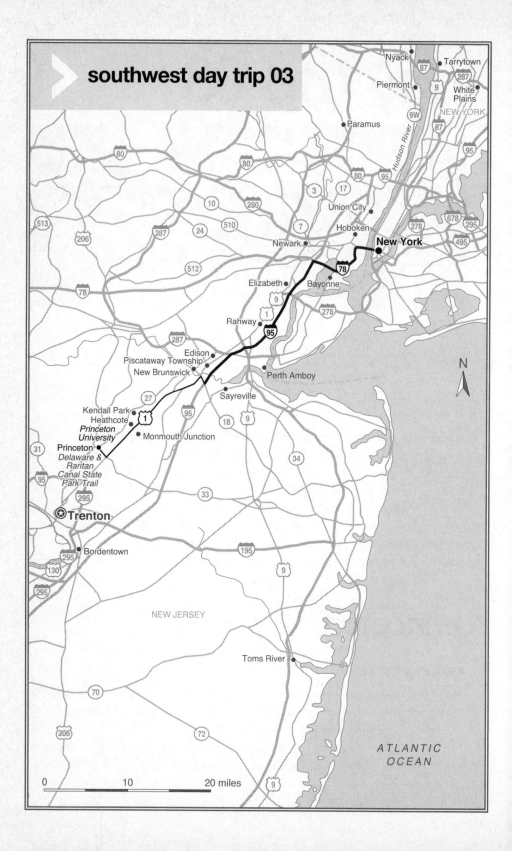

US 1 S in New Brunswick. Take a right on CR 571/Washington Road, which takes you right into town.

where to go

Delaware and Raritan Canal State Park. 145 Maple Rd., Princeton; (609) 924-5705. This 70-mile park is broken into two sections—the main canal and the feeder canal—and is a popular recreational area for anyone interested in the outdoors. Visitors can jog the towpaths, go horseback riding, or fish in designated areas. Rent a bike from **Kopps** bike shop, the oldest in America (http://koppscycle.net) and ride along the canal. You can also rent a canoe from **Princeton Canoe Rental** (609-452-2403) and canoe along the canal. But don't go on a muggy day as the canal is full of flies.

McCarter Theatre. 91 University Place, Princeton; (609) 258-2787. Staging more than 200 performances a year, from dance to play to music, the McCarter Theatre is a preview spot for many shows that go to Broadway. The theater is committed to re-imagining classic works as well as staging new works by emerging writers. The theater is located just across from the train station.

Onsen Spa. 4451 NJ 27, Princeton; (609) 924-4800. Worth a day trip for the spa alone, Onsen Spa is one of the most authentic Japanese spas outside of Japan and is often filled with Japanese families on the weekend. To get here, you must have a car as a taxi ride from the heart of Princeton is pretty expensive. If you want to splurge, it's well worth the effort as the outdoor soaking tubs in winter offer a wonderful respite from the stress of the city. The massages are even better than ones found in pricier Manhattan hotel spas.

Princeton Public Library. 65 Witherspoon St., Princeton; (609) 924-9529. Located on a lovely square, the Princeton Public Library is worth a visit for its welcoming coffee shop and outdoor decks on which to relax and read. The library also sells used books, and you might come across some great finds.

Princeton University Art Museum. McCormick Hall, Nassau Street, Princeton; (609) 258-3788. Most university art museums don't have as vast a collection. The Princeton University Art Museum boasts a variety of art and antiquities from the Americas to Europe to Asia. The specialties are Chinese figures, Islamic art, and pre-Columbian art as well as 20th century sculpture from the likes of Pablo Picasso, Henry Moore, and Alexander Calder.

Terhune Orchards. 330 Cold Soil Rd., Princeton; (609) 924-2310. One of Princeton's nicest family-run farms. Visitors can go apple, cherry, berry, flower, and pumpkin picking on the 200-acre estate. Terhune also sells homemade cider and pies, and organizes read & pick excursions for the whole family.

"there's something in the water . . . "

Everyone knows that New York, Detroit, Los Angeles, and Athens, Georgia, are music meccas. Just think of the number of musicians that have hailed from those cities. But did you know you can add tony Princeton to that list? From country musician Steve "Buddy" Miller to Mary Chapin Carpenter to John Popper of Blues Traveler to Chris Barron of Spin Doctors to Trey Anastasio of Phish, Princeton has seen its fair share of creative voices. While nowhere near the level of those bigger towns, the music departments of Princeton Day School and Princeton High School must be encouraging local talent to follow their dreams. It's just another example of how music and arts education funding is so important, no matter the location of the school.

where to shop

Jazams. 25 Palmer Sq. East, Princeton; (609) 924-8697. Jazams is one of the best toy stores in the country. The store has train sets that kids can play with, books in different languages, great games for every age, and books that will tempt even adult readers. The shop is a great spot to nurture your inner child.

Joy Cards. 6 Chambers St., Princeton; (609) 430-0333. People from Philly and New York consider Joy Cards a must-stop shop for all their stationery and card needs. The shop is small but packs a punch. The unique card selection is top notch, and you can find something for any occasion. The shop also has a great selection of initiations and announcements cards for weddings, engagements, and other events.

Zoe. 11 Hulfish St., Princeton; (609) 497-0704. A Princeton outpost of a cool Brooklyn boutique. Zoe features a plethora of up-and-coming designers as well as high-profile brands such as Lanvin, Stella McCartney, and Miu Miu. Sales occur often and are fantastic.

where to eat

Bent Spoon. 35 Palmer Sq. West, Princeton; (609) 924-2368. Jam-packed with ice-cream aficionados year-round, Bent Spoon is one of the finest ice-cream parlors in the northeast. Besides classic flavors such as chocolate, vanilla, and chocolate chip, Bent Spoon creates seasonal flavors based on fruit grown from local farms. In the summer, the lines go around the block. $.

Mediterra. 29 Hulfish St., Princeton; (609) 252-9680. Located on lovely Palmer Square, Mediterra showcases the cuisine of 21 nations on the Mediterranean Sea. Head here for savory paella or tasty calamari. Stay for a glass of wine. The taverna is a great place at which to imbibe a glass of good wine and enjoy a small plate. It's also a great spot at which to watch soccer or football on a Sun afternoon. Open for lunch and dinner seven days a week. $$.

where to stay

Inn at Glencairn. 3301 Lawrenceville Rd., Princeton; (609) 497-1737. Nestled on several bucolic acres, 3 miles from downtown Princeton, the Inn at Glencairn has 5 unique guest rooms, elegantly furnished without kitschy afghans or patchwork quilts. The care and consideration giving into designing this Georgian manse is on display. Rooms boast en suite bathrooms, flatscreen TVs, feather beds, Egyptian cotton linens, LATHER bath products, and Frette robes. Breakfasts are hearty, and you won't feel sluggish after eating here: all breakfast items are organically sourced. The hotel offers discounts for business travelers and stay and spa packages for couples. $$$.

Nassau Inn. 10 Palmer Sq., Princeton; (609) 921-7500. This Palmer Square hotel has long been a local favorite for its friendly service and comfortable, yet elegant lodgings. The federal structure has 203 room, 7 of which are specialty suites, some wheelchair accessible. The hotel runs specials throughout the year and also runs the Yankee Doodle Tap Room on the premises. $$$.

appendix:
festivals & celebrations

Festivals abound around the Tri-state area and Pennsylvania, but here are some you may not be familiar with. Visit the state Tourism Bureaus for a list of current events: **I Love New York** (www.iloveny.com); **Visit Connecticut** (888-CTVISIT; www.ctvisit.com); **New Jersey Tourism** (800-VISITNJ; www.visitnj.org); **Visit Pennsylvania** (800-VisitPA; www.visitpa.com).

january

Philagrafika is Philadelphia's four-month-long contemporary and print arts festival (it runs from late Jan to early Apr) held at more than 50 venues around the city. Most exhibitions are free but a few museums in the area do charge admission. www.philagrafika.org. (215) 557-8433.

february

Feel the love in lovely Clinton at the **Sweetheart Week and Food Drive.** Visitors can enter to win great prizes as well as help the area needy. www.clintonguild.com.

march

Ballard Park plays host to Ridgefield's **St. Patrick's Day Scavenger Hunt.** Kids learn about Irish folklore and Ridgefield history, and every child goes home with a prize no matter the outcome of the hunt. www.ridgefielddiscovery.org.

Every March 14, Princeton celebrates Albert Einstein's birth by throwing the **Princeton Pi Day** and **Einstein's Birthday Party.** If you look closely you'll get the reference to pie (hint, it's in the numerical designation of the birthday). Einstein lived in Princeton for 20 years, and the town celebrates with pie judging and pi recitation contests. www.visitprinceton.org.

april

Grab the kids and your paper, plastic, or fabric kite and head to **Art's Point** in tony Greenwich for the annual Kite Flying Festival. www.greenwicharts.org.

Lambertville's annual **Shad Festival** celebrates the city, the region's art, and the town's favorite fish, the shad (shad fishing was a huge industry during the town's history). The town celebrates with art stalls, food courts, face painting for the kids, and a poster auction. www.lambertville.org.

may

Kids of all ages head to Wildwoods, New Jersey, for the **International Kite Festival,** which occurs every year during the last weekend of the month. Kite flying competitions and lunar kite displays wow everyone who heads to the beach town before the summer begins.

Bethlehem's 10-day **Musikfest** attracts more than a million people and is considered one of the largest outdoor concerts in the country with more than 500 performers.

The annual **Iris Festival** in Bordentown boasts antiques, artists, jazz musicians, and an Iris grower's competition, *natch.* Guests should end their visit with a tour of the **Franklin Carr Memorial Iris Garden** in Flynn Park. (609) 298-8066; www.downtownbordentown.com.

Held in May, June, and October, **Nyack Street Fair** boasts antiques vendors, food stalls, and children's play areas. www.pjspromotions.com.

The **Brandywine River Blues Festival** is one of Philadelphia's best events of the year. Rock out to great blues at Chaddsford Winery in nearby Chaddsford, Pennsylvania. www.thebrandywine.com.

june

Lower Main Street plays host to a variety of kid-centric arts and crafts activities at Clinton's **Art in the Open: A Children's Outdoor Art Festival**. www.clintonnj.gov.

The Hartford Symphony Orchestra performs classic pieces in the beautiful outdoors at the **Talcott Mountain Music Festival** in Simsbury from late June to late July. www .hartfordsymphony.org.

For more than five decades, visitors have flocked to the **Mattituck Lions Strawberry Festival** for strawberries at their peak and to check out the wares of more than 100 vendors. www.mattituckstrawberryfestival.org.

From late June to early August, chamber music, jazz, bluegrass, and other musical genres get top billing at Caramoor's annual **International Music Festival** in Katonah. www.caramoor.org.

Head to Riverfront Park for the Beacon Sloop Club's annual **Strawberry Festival.** Food, music, and crafts are for sale. All proceed benefit the organization. www.cityofbeacon .org.

For three months, Cold Spring and Garrison host the **Hudson Valley Shakespeare Festival** with reenactments, readings, and performances of Shakespeare plays. www .hvshakespeare.org.

Cuban-born salsa singer **Celia Cruz,** the darling of Union City, gets her own tribute festival every year at her namesake park. www.celiacruz.com.

july

For three nights in mid July, jazz fanatics head to the small town of Burlington for the **Burlington Jazz, Blues and Heritage Festival.** The festival is noteworthy for showcasing the next generation of stars as well as icons such as Spyro Gyra. www.burlingtonjazzblues-heritagefest.org.

Things get racy at the **Fire Island Drag Queen Invasion,** which celebrates gay pride as well as gay rights. www.fireislandinvasion.com.

The grand Vanderbilt Museum in Centerport celebrates its **Independence Festival.** Enjoy crafts, Shakespeare plays, reptiles, and planetarium sky shows. www.vanderbilt museum.org.

Storm the Bastille in Frenchtown in mid-July. **Bastille Day** incorporates street performers, clowns, music, and movie screenings in a weekendlong celebration. (908) 996-7080.

Artisans from around the country display their wares at Haddonfield's annual **Fine Arts and Crafts Festival,** which is almost two decades old. Area restaurants set up stalls, and musicians treat visitors to energetic tunes. www.haddonfieldnj.com.

Food and music lovers will enjoy the three-day **New Jersey State Barbecue Championship and Anglesea Blues Festival** (Wildwoods Barbecue and Blues Festival). Check out the wing challenge or the iron chef dessert and sauce contest.

august

New Hope's **Midsummer Madness Weekend** features a town-wide red tag sale as well as an auto show.

september

Well-known folk acts take center stage at the **Connecticut Folk Festival and Green Expo.** The festival teaches visitors how to live greener, healthier lives. www.ctfolk.com.

Labor Day weekend in Litchfield is a day of celebration. **A Taste of the Litchfield Hills** is a food and wine festival that attracts thousands of food and wine lovers from the tri-state area. www.litchfieldfestivals.com.

Sands Point Preserve hosts the **Medieval Festival** for two consecutive weekends. A tented medieval village is the centerpiece as participants joust and compete in archery competitions. www.kingdomofacre.org.

Bedford Hills' **Feed Me Fresh Benefit** supports Mt. Kisco's Child Care Center and promotes sustainable nutrition. www.mkdcc.org.

The Blauvelt Lions free **Applefest** showcases apple pastries as well as pony rides, craft stalls, and other fun excursions. (845) 365-8293.

october

Situated in and around lovely Meetinghouse Square, **Historic Fallsington Day** boasts city residents resplendent in period costumes, Native American dancers, quill demonstrations, and puppeteers. www.historicfallsington.org.

The spooky towns of Sleepy Hollow and Tarrytown play host to a number of ghostly events during October. The most enjoyable is **Legend Weekend,** which has child-friendly events during the day but gets suitably eerie and macabre during the evening. (914) 631-8200; www.hudsonvalley.org.

The Port Jervis Annual **Fall Foliage Festival Car Show** is a great way to check out vintage and restored cars as they duke it out for best in category. (845) 856-4310; www.cruzinport.com.

Thousands head to the seaside town of Oyster Bay for **Oyster Festival** for seafood stalls, live music, and great desserts. Free shuttle buses run from two LIRR stops. www.theoysterfestival.org.

Good food and even better wine take center stage at Millbrook Vineyards & Winery annual **Harvest Party.** www.millbrookwine.com.

Wish St. Patrick's Day was twice a year? Head to the **Aoh Irish Day Parade and Festival** in Long Beach for crafts, food, and green beer. www.longbeachny.org.

Benmarl Winery in Marlboro hosts the annual **Harvest Grape Stomping Festival.** Enjoy live music, grape stomping, hay rides, and more. www.benmarl.com.

Enjoy live music, pumpkin-carving, pie-eating, scarecrow-design, and costume contests at Barryville's annual **Pumpkin Fest.** (845) 557-6500; www.barryvilleny.com/event/pumpkinfest.html.

Dress up your pet and join in the Warwick Valley Humane Society's Annual **Walkathon and Howl-o-ween Pet Costume Parade,** which raises much needed funds for the animal organization.

Join your fellow booklovers for the **Collingswood Book Festival,** the largest literary event in the region. www.collingswood.com.

november

The Friday after Thanksgiving, Old Saint Nick descends from the roof of Borough Hall by way of the Collingswood Fire Department's ladder truck. The downtown is lit up just in time for the **Collingswood Holiday Parade,** considered one of the most fun events in the region. www.collingswood.com.

Sweet lovers love the **Kent Gingerbread Festival** every November and December. The quaint village boasts baking classes, gingerbread house competitions, tree lighting, and singing. Free. www.kentct.com.

december

Say sayonara to another year gone at **New Year's Eve Under the Stars** at Custer Institute and Observatory in Southold. Enjoy hors d'oeuvres, drinks, and champagne toasts while gazing at the heavens through powerful telescopes. www.custerobservatory.org.

Two Christmas events in Nazareth are iconic. The annual **Lovefeast** celebrates the city's birth as well as the formation of the American Moravian church. Christmas in Nazareth features traditional carolers, Santa Claus, and a manger scene. www.moravianhistorical society.org.

Every year, Hoboken celebrates the birthday of its favorite son. Hoboken city clerk Jimmy Farina organizes the **Frank Sinatra Birthday Bash** complete with cake. There are other events around the city commemorating the birth of Ol' Blue Eyes.

index